Jesus, Fill My Heart & Home

D1557365

Meredith Curtis

ISBN-13:978-1523956128

DEDICATION

This book is dedicated to Julianna Sheree Curtis who bakes, cooks, creates, crafts, and decorates with a joyful heart, creating a warm, loving environment for all to enjoy! I am grateful that you ask God to fill you up with His Presence—it overflows to everyone around you!

CONTENTS

ACKNOWLEDGMENTS

Thank you to Laura for all your graphic design work on the front and back covers, as well as all your help with layout and editing.

Thank you to all the ladies, young and old, who have been through this Bible study and offered suggestions, feedback, and encouragement. .

1 MASKS, MAKEOVERS, & THE NATURAL LOOK

You are invited to a formal dinner, where important dignitaries will be dining with you. What will you wear? You are going to clean the garage out. What will you wear? We are used to putting on different clothing for different situations.

When it comes to our faces, we think in the same way. Most of us don't wear make-up to bed, but we do wear it on a date with our husband or for the annual family photo shoot. We change our "look" or face for different situations.

When it comes to our spiritual life, do we wear masks or just keep the "natural look" and allow others to see the "real thing?" Let's take a look at masks, the "natural look," and the possibility of a make-over. Get ready for a journey that will take you deeper in your walk with the Lord and make you more effective in sharing His Presence with others! This week you will learn to effectively use God's mirror.

Read I Thessalonians 2:1-8

Was Paul's visit to Thessalonica a success or failure?

What about the previous visit to Philippi?

What happened in Philippi?

Paul has written this letter with Silas and Timothy, who helped him plant the church in Thessalonica. He says that after the rough time in Philippi, they **dared** to tell the Thessalonians the Gospel, or Good News about Jesus!

Have you ever faced opposition in declaring the Good News about Jesus? Maybe you have faced opposition in trying to live a godly life that honors the Lord. Maybe people have questioned your behavior ("But, everyone else is…"), ideals ("No one believes that anymore!"), or attitude ("Why are you always so happy? Are you UP to something?"). Take heart, Jesus promised his followers that if they persecuted Him, they will persecute His followers too! "They," meaning people who are not following God, can make things difficult, so we must start out by refusing to try to make "them" happy. That was how Paul could go on to Thessalonica and lead so many to Christ!

Who does Paul try to please?

Evidently, some others who were preaching the Gospel tried to use preaching as a way to flatter the Thessalonians and trick them out of their money. We, of course, never see that today. Oops—I'm being sarcastic! Seriously, it's nothing new, there are always black sheep dressed as shepherds of God, who are only out to "fleece the flock." Pastors who take advantage of God's people will face God's judgment.

What about you and me? Do we try to flatter people so that we can get our way? Do we try to hide our motives so that we can manipulate other? (Do we ever trick our husbands, children, or friends so that they will do what we want?) Do we ever wear masks, pretending to be someone we are not?

Paul said that he never wore a mask to cover up greed.

What masks do Christians wear?

What masks do you sometimes wear? (Who or what do you pretend to be)

What are you trying to "cover up" by wearing a mask?

Instead of wearing a mask or using flattery, what did Paul do?

How will pleasing God, instead of people, set you free from masks and flattery?

How do we know what pleases God?

Read Hebrews 4:12-13

Describe The Word of God.

Read James 1:22-25

If you look in a mirror and discover that your hair is messy and your shirt's buttons are mis-matched, what happens if you forget all about it?

What if you make adjustments to your hair, but not your buttons?

What if you fix everything, look again in the mirror and fix anything else you discover?

How is the Bible like a mirror?

Should We Wear Masks? Keep the "Natural Look"? Get a Makeover?

Once we see ourselves in the mirror, we have three choices. We can keep the "natural look," wear a mask, or have a makeover. We are tempted to wear masks to hide who we really are. We don't want people to see our flaws. We want to project an image that isn't really who we are, but rather who we dream of being.

Do you ever find yourself saying the following things or thinking them to yourself?

"I won't let anyone know how I **really** feel inside"

"There is an image I must maintain"

"The show must go on"

"It's not who you are, but who people think you are that matters"

If so, you may be a mask wearer!

Keeping the "Natural Look"

If you find yourself saying or thinking the following things to excuse bad behavior, you may be one who wants to keep the "natural look."

"This is just who I am"

"I can't help it—it's the way God made me"

"It's my spiritual gift of prophecy"

"Being bossy is just my personality"

Masks are bad things to wear when you are a Christian. We are to be authentic, transparent, and humble, willing to let others see us as we really are. However, "the natural look" can be just as bad, when we use it as an excuse to stay the same and never change. We don't keep on sinning once we come to know Jesus! We repent and get rid of sin. We make radical changes in our demeanor, lifestyle, and words! There is no going back. We are always moving forward!

A woman named Susie was bossy, demanding, and rude. She was a Christian, but did not want others to "step on her" or take "advantage of her." She loved to share her opinion with others in a way that was forceful and rude. She came to see me because she was lonely and confessed that she possessed no friends. "No wonder!" I wanted to retort, but I held my tongue. I gently addressed her overbearing personality and to my surprise, she was quite aware of it. "It's just my gifting," she rationalized. "It's the way God made me."

God goes not give us a "gifting" that is ungodly. It is not holy to be rude, bossy, opinionated, or overbearing. Susie was determined to wear the "natural look" even after a look into God's mirror.

Whether we wear a mask or refuse to change the "natural look," what we really need is help from our Heavenly Father. What we really need is to powerful transformation by the Word of God!

What About a Makeover?

Do you ever find yourself saying the following things or thinking them to yourself?

"I wish I was a different person"

"I wish I felt that way"

"I wish I could be bold and friendly"

"I wish God would change me from the inside out"

If so, you are in a great place! Humble, teachable, and ready for God's makeover. When my friend, Sarah, first gave her life to Jesus, she came to me and asked how she could grow in the Lord. I encouraged her to read Scripture, pray, listen to worship CDs, spend time with other believers and take notes during the sermons. Within a month, she was back. "What else can I do?" she asked. Her heart was to press in and grow closer to the Lord. Today she is a lovely woman of God, seeking Him with all of her heart. She's had a make-over!

How Do We Use God's Mirror?

The Bible is the mirror we use to experience God's makeover. His power will transform our lives! We come in humility to the Scriptures, expecting God to reveal things we need to learn and adjustments we need to make.

Instead of trying to get through our Bible reading quickly each day, we slow down and read the Scriptures devotionally. We let the Spirit show us when to linger over a verse. Realize that all of us have blind spots. The Word of God can shine on those blind spots and reveal them, just as a full-length mirror can reveal a little tummy bulge that you didn't realize you had acquired.

Before you begin to read the Bible each morning, pray first. Ask the Holy Spirit to teach you and change you. Then write down whatever "stands out" to you in the passage you are reading. Remind yourself throughout the day of what you read in your Quiet Time. You can do this by sharing it with a friend or prayer partner, writing it on a note and glancing at it periodically, or talking to God about it all day. Better yet, do all three!

A fun thing to do is to pick out a Scripture passage (Romans 12 or Ephesians 4 are great for this!) Simply read the passage until you come across something that you are doing that you should **not** do, or something you **should** do that you are not doing. Then pray, asking God to change you!

Balanced Diet

Just as we need a balanced diet of food to maintain optimal health, we also need a balanced diet of God's Word. The **whole** Bible is good for us, not just our favorite books! Make it your ambition to read through the New Testament once a year and the Old Testament every three years. This way, you are reading **all** of the Scriptures, not just some.

We also need a balance of hearing, reading, studying, memorizing and meditating on the Word of God.

Listen, Read, & Study

We listen to Scripture in church and in family devotions. We read our Bibles in our Quiet Times. In-depth study of God's Word, especially inductive Bible studies, are a helpful addition to our balanced diet. Inductive Bible studies use the three part method of observation, interpretation, and application.

When we **observe** a passage, we ask:

- "Who wrote this?"
- "Who is talking or doing something in the passage?"
- "What action or dialogue is taking place?"
- "What is the subject of the passage?"
- "Where is all this happening?"

When we **interpret** a passage, we ask:

- "Why is this being talked about?"

- "How does this relate to the previous chapter, the rest of the book and the entire Bible?"
- "What are the cultural implications of what is being said or done?"
- "Why are particular words and phrases used?"

When we **apply** a passage, we ask:

- "What does this have to say to me?"
- "How can I live this out in my life?"

Memorize & Meditate!

To meditate on Scripture, we must first memorize it! We pick out a verse or passage and carefully memorize it word for word. Once it is in our memory banks, we take it out and think about it as we drive, wash dishes, bake a cake, or take a walk. We simply allow our mind to focus on this portion of Scripture…what does it mean? Why are these particular words used? What does this passage reveal about God? What does it reveal about my heart?

The reason we memorize carefully word by word, verse by verse, is that it allows us to understand God's heart, mind and thought structures. We get a glimpse into the "Mind of Christ!" Once we have the verse memorized, we can personalize it. We can pray the Scriptures over our lives. Here is a prayer based on Psalm 37:3-7.

Lord, Your Word says that if I delight myself in You, you will give me the desires of my heart. Jesus, my desire is for you. Teach me to delight myself in you.

What we think determines how we feel and what we do. So much of the battle against fear, doubt, temptation, and defeat takes place in our minds. It is a good thing to get rid of futile thought patterns and replace them with God's way of thinking! Remember that the Word of God is powerful and will cleanse, sanctify, instruct and transform us. If you seriously begin to memorize and meditate on the Scriptures, you will **never** be the same!

When Mike and I began courting, he suggested that we memorize

Scripture together.

"Let's memorize Romans 12 for next week," he suggested.

"Which verse?" I queried.

"The whole chapter!" he replied.

Gulp! I wasn't prepared for that answer, but I was in love, so I memorized Romans 12! Wow! What an exciting month followed, as everywhere I went, God made this passage alive in my heart and life. I was hooked on memorizing and meditating on Scripture! Attitudes changed. People that were hard to love became dear to my heart. I was having a make-over!

There are so many wonderful passages and verses! Where should you begin?! Start with verses and move on to passages. Here are a few suggestions.

James 3 Wisdom/the Tongue

Romans 12:9-18 Relationships in the Church

Romans 8 Our Inheritance in Christ!

Psalm 139 Positive self-image

I Peter 3:1-8 Husband & Wife Relationships

Luke 11:1-11 Prayer

Psalm 23 God's Loving Care

I Corinthians 13 Love

John 15 Abiding

Psalm 91 God's Protection

Psalm 1 Meditating on God's Word

Isaiah 53 Jesus Christ the Messiah

Psalm 11 God's Provision & Protection

Ephesians 6:10-18 Spiritual Warfare

On the next page I have provided you with a personal Bible study worksheet. This guide will help you dig a little deeper into God's Word. As you receive greater insight, you will be able to apply what you study to your own life. As you apply Scripture to your life, you will experience God's power, a heavenly makeover. It is so exciting to study God's Word!

Personal Bible Study Sheet

Book & Chapter: Date:

Key verse to memorize:

Observations (interesting things you notice about people, place, time, atmosphere, situation, etc.:

Choose a title for each paragraph:

How are the paragraphs related to each other? (Similarities, contrasts, cause and effect)

What meaning or truth does each connection point out?

What is the big truth this passage is teaching? Write it in one sentence.

What is the main thing the Lord is saying to me through this chapter? (Something to obey? A truth about Him I can rejoice in? A promise I can take for a situation I'm in?)

Further Insights:

Other related passages (Search for related texts by cross reference and concordance):

2 ABIDING IN GOD'S WORD

We are still on the topic of God's Word, but now we are going to talk about the role of the Bible in abiding in Christ. We will talk about abiding in Him and letting His Word abide in us. First, get a dictionary out and let's look up these words. I know that they are simple words. But looking up words can give us deeper insight in their meaning and thus, into the passage we are studying.

Abiding & Bearing Fruit Vocabulary

Define the following words:

Vine:

Gardener:

Branches:

Bear (produce):

Fruit:

Prune:

Clean:

Abide/Dwell/Live in:

Joy:

Love:

Business:

Friend:

Now, let's move into the passage we will focus on several times in our journey through abiding. Depending on the version you use, your Bible may use the word 'abide,' 'dwell,' or 'remain.' Each word expresses the same idea—to *make your home in*. Let's look more closely at this wonderful passage.

John 15 is located right in the middle of John 13-18, chapters that reveal the events that took place on the night of Jesus' arrest. First, there is the Last Supper, in John 13 and 14, where Jesus celebrates the Passover with his disciples, explaining how He fulfills the Passover Feast. In the upper room, he institutes communion which the church practices to this day, remembering His death and resurrection. He also washed the disciples' feet, demonstrating humility and love, and taught them about the Holy Spirit. We will see in later weeks how important the Holy Spirit is in this life of abiding. When this time is finished, the disciples sing a hymn, leave, and head to the Garden of Gethsemane. I can just see Jesus reaching up and holding the branch of a grapevine while He explained these beautiful truths in the passage we are about to read. Keep in mind, as you look at this passage, that Jesus is about to pray, be arrested, and go to the cross for our sins.

Read John 15:1-4

There are three roles mentioned in this passage. What are they? Who fulfills each role?

Role #1   **Role #2**   **Role #3**

What is our purpose as a branch? What is the Gardner looking for in our lives?

What is our responsibility as a branch?

Think of a grapevine or fruit tree. Do you see the branches struggling and straining to bear fruit? It is the Gardner who plants, waters, feeds, weeds and prunes his vines and trees.

Why does a gardener prune the plants in his garden?

Does he only prune the dead limbs away? Or does he cut back fruitful branches too?

What is the purpose of pruning in our spiritual lives?

What do you think pruning looks like?

How does the "Mirror of God" (Bible) help to prune our lives?

Read John 15:5-8

What does it mean to have God's Word **abide** in us?

How can God's Word abide in your heart even more than it already does?

Galatians 5:22-23

By the way, this is the fruit that the Gardener, your Heavenly Father, is looking for. List the Fruit of the Spirit.

John 15:9-17

One aspect of abiding is obedience. When the Word of God's abides in us, we obey it! Why does obedience lead to JOY?

What is the Father's business? How were the disciples involved with Jesus in His Father's business?

What business has Father delegated to us?

What is the difference between a tree and a vine? List these differences below.

Tree   **Vine**

Our purpose as a branch is to bear fruit. This fruit (love, joy, peace, patience, kindness, goodness, gentleness, faithfulness, and self-control) is really the Character of God Himself, replacing our own character. Jesus begins to live His life through us in greater and greater ways. People see us changing and becoming more like Him.

Love, Joy, Peace, Patience, Kindness, Goodness, Gentleness, Faithfulness, & Self-Control

Producing fruit is not something that we can do on our own. Our responsibility as a branch is to remain, or abide, in the vine. We must stay connected! As we stay connected to Him, fruit blossoms forth from the inside of our hearts to the outside of our lives. Don't focus on striving to produce fruit. The ultimate secret of abiding is complete surrender to God! We allow Him to do what He wants, when He wants, however He wants, in our lives. It is His agenda, not our own. Our delight becomes His Presence, not His blessings.

God desires a close relationship with us and to see godly character in our lives. Of course, our Heavenly Gardener prunes away sin! He gets rid of anything that is disobedient to the will and Word of God. When we use the Bible as a mirror, sin is revealed, and we can repent, turning away from it. In this way, Scripture is used to prune us.

Our Heavenly Father might also prune away **good** things in our life, so that we will press in closer to Him. Sometimes so we can focus on areas of our life that need to grow stronger in the Lord, Jesus will prune away an activity or person that is dear to us. After pruning, we become more fruitful! Just as the branch grows back, often fresh growth occurs and we move back into those areas of ministry or friendships again.

The Ultimate Secret of Abiding: Complete Surrender to God!

Jesus lived His life completely focused on the Father's agenda, His business. He came to earth to rescue men and women from every nation, tribe and tongue, bringing them together to be His church. He lived for the will of God, never His personal agenda. The difference between a vine and a tree is that a tree stays in one place whereas a vine can go all over the place. As long as the roots are strong, a vine can travel. Like a vine, we can go wherever the Lord leads us, as long as we are firmly rooted in Jesus.

The Father's business is the Great Commission: making disciples for Jesus and building His church! His commands involve love that transforms the heart and life of everyone who believes in Jesus. This is our business too if we are truly friends of God. We are "all about" making disciples and loving people in His Name. In that way, we are fulfilling God's purpose, surrendered to Him!

The Word of God can abide in us through Bible reading, Bible study, Bible memorization, Bible meditation, and hearing the Bible read aloud. The more we fill our lives with Scripture, the more we are able to recognize the voice of the Lord when the Holy Spirit speaks to our hearts. We will recognize His voice because it will always line up with the Word of God. Don't forget to keep looking into "His Mirror"!

10 Ways to Fill our Lives with The Word of God!

1. Read each day **aloud**!

2. Write down Bible verses on index cards, decorate, and put in prominent places.

3. Type up Scripture verses and/or passages on computer. Or write them in your prettiest handwriting.

4. Listen to the Bible on CDs. Or listen to someone else read Scripture aloud.

5. Listen to Worship CDs that have Scripture verses or psalms set to music. Sing the old hymns—many are taken right from the Bible!

6. Read the Bible to children (or adults) aloud with extra expression. Add drama to your voice and facial expressions.

7. Stash Bibles all around the house—read when you can! Put them in the kitchen, family room, bathroom, bedrooms, and in the car!

8. Get away once in awhile for three hours or more to read the Bible and pray!

9. Focus on one verse or passage each week or each month.

    • Read it aloud.

    • Memorize part or all of it (children can do this too!)

    • Write it down and decorate the paper it's written on.

    • Explain the verse to another person.

    • Ponder the words, their meanings, and application.

10. Start reading a passage—ask the Holy Spirit to stop you at the verse He wants to teach you about. When He stops you, use the verse to examine your heart and behavior. Pray for God's help to apply the verse to your life!

10 Benefits from Filling our Lives with The Word of God!

1. When we meditate on God's Word, the result is bearing fruit, prospering, and health. (Psalm 1)

2. When we meditate day and night on and obey God's Word, we will experience success. (Joshua 1:8)

3. The Bible has the power to change our lives! When we memorize verses and passages, we are able to avoid sin. (Psalm 119:9-11)

4. We need to be "washed with water" through the Word. Scripture washes away the crud in our lives. (Ephesians 5:25-27)

5. Knowledge is a building block that, along with the other building blocks, leads to a changed life that is productive and effective. (II Peter 1:5-8)

6. The Bible is filled with God's promises which give us everything we need for life and godliness, by allowing us to participate in the divine nature and escape the corruption of the world! (II Peter 1:3-4)

7. His Word is flawless! We can find refuge in His promises, His ways and His truth! (Proverbs 30:5-6)

8. His ways and thoughts, revealed in His Word, are higher than our ways and thoughts. His Word, when sent forth accomplishes it purpose! The Scriptures can't help but **work**! (Isaiah 55:9-11)

9. The Bible equips us for every good work and makes us wise for salvation. We are encouraged, rebuked, corrected and trained by it! We are able to go out, kick in the gates of hell to rescue captives to sin, and live victorious lives as we read, obey, study, memorize, and meditate on Scripture! (II Timothy 3:15-17)

10. The Word of God is like spiritual milk for newborn babies, helping us to grow up in our salvation. We will taste and see that the Lord is good! It also purifies us, creating love in our hearts for other believers! (I Peter 1:22-3:3)

If God's Word is abiding in me, then it is alive and in control in every area of my life. This requires that I take His Word very seriously, knowing that it is TRUE, knowing that it WORKS, knowing that it will draw me deeper into this life of abiding. If God's Word is truly abiding in me, then everything will be different. People should be able to just take one look at me and see the goodness and truth found in the Scriptures, the promises fulfilled, the Biblical principles working in real life situations. Letting God's Word abide in me doesn't just change me, it changes the people around me too!

3 AM I PRAYING LOUD ENOUGH FOR GOD TO HEAR ME?

Have you ever felt that your prayers were "bouncing off the ceiling" or somehow not quite getting through the Heavenly circuit? This passage on prayer may be just what you need to clear up any misunderstanding or misperceptions on your part. God is eager to hear your prayers and bless you because He loves you.

Read Luke 11:1-13

What is the main topic of this passage?

What famous prayer is quoted by Jesus, as He teaches His disciples to pray?

We are going to look at this passage in four sections:

1. Jesus teaches the disciples the "Lord's Prayer."
2. Jesus' parable of the bold, almost impertinent, seeker of bread.
3. Jesus' command to ask, seek, and knock.
4. Jesus' illustration of fathers giving good gifts to their children.

Read Luke 11:1-4   (also see Matthew 6:9-13)

"Our Father" Jesus tells His disciples to address God as "Father," a personal and intimate title.

How is God a "Father" to His children?

Addressing prayers to "Father God" gives us confidence that He will listen because fathers care about their children. List all the things that God cares about in your life.

Stop right now and address God as your Father who loves you!

"Hallowed be Thy Name"

"Hallowed" means to set apart as holy or regard with great reverence!

The beginning of the "Lord's Prayer" is a declaration that God is worthy!

We should worship Him.

List all the things you love about God.

Stop right now and worship God—tell Him how wonderful He is!

"Thy Kingdom come, Thy will be done; on earth as it is in Heaven!" (From Matthew 6:9) is a request for God's perfect will to be done on earth. In Heaven there is only truth, holiness, joy, purity, and obedience. What things would need to change in this world so that this world could be like Heaven?

What things in your world would change if God's kingdom power and perfect will arrived?

Stop right now and pray for God's will to be done in your life.

"Give us this day our daily bread"

What needs do you have?

How can God provide?

List all your needs.

Stop right now and pray for needs in your life and those you love. Thank Him for providing faithfully.

"Forgive us our sins as we forgive those who sin against us"

What sins have been committed against you?

Who do you still need to forgive from the past and the present?

 Stop right now and forgive them.

What sins have you committed?

What things have you left undone? What attitudes have been negative? What words have you spoken that you shouldn't have said?

 Stop right now and repent. Ask God to forgive you.

"And lead us not into temptation, but deliver us from evil"

What temptations do you face?

Stop and pray for God's help in resisting temptation and overcoming bad habits.

The "Lord's Prayer is a pattern for your own prayer life! It covers all the bases that need to be covered! We don't have to say the "Lord's Prayer" every morning in our Quiet Times, but if you don't have it memorized—then just do it! When you don't know how to pray, use this as your pattern.

Our Father, who art in Heaven

Hallowed be Thy Name; Thy Kingdom come, Thy will be done

On earth as it is in Heaven! Give us this day our daily bread;

Forgive us our sins as we forgive those who sin against us;

Lead us not into temptation, but deliver us from evil;

For Thine is the Kingdom and the Glory; Forever and ever;

Amen.

Read Luke 11:5-8

Jesus continues to teach on prayer by sharing a story about a man who needs bread.

Why does the man in the story need bread?

What time is it?

Do you borrow things from people at midnight?

The audacity of this man is commended by Jesus. Are you bold and daring in your prayer life?

Are things you are afraid to ask God for?   What are you afraid to ask for?

What can you do to be more tenacious and determined in your prayer life?

Do you have any pressing needs right now?   What are your pressing needs?

 Stop and pray boldly for your pressing needs.

Read Luke 11:9-10

What happens to those who ask?

What happens to those who seek?

What happens to those who knock?

What are you asking for?

What are you seeking?

What doors are you knocking on?

 Stop, ask, seek and knock!

Read Luke 11:11-13

Do most fathers willingly harm their children?

Why do fathers give good gifts to their children?

Even though earthly fathers are evil because mankind is a fallen race, they still want to bless their children with good gifts. Imagine how much more our Heavenly Father, who is Perfect Love, wants to bless you! He wants to lavish us with His blessings. God even wants to give us **Himself**, the Holy Spirit! His heart is kind, benevolent, and compassionate.

What gifts do you want to receive from God?

Will God give you something that is bad for you?

Why do you think God sometimes says, "No"?

The nature of God is to give. Jesus came to serve, redeem, ransom, and set free captives who rejected His Lordship. He died for His enemies. The Lord's heart is to bless us. Our need is to cry out to Him, to pour our hearts out boldly with a determination that we are going to ask Him for the desires of our heart!

Pressing needs can be overwhelming, but need to lead us to prayer. Prayer strengthens our relationship with Jesus! The next time you have a pressing need, see it as a gift from God to draw you closer to Himself through prayer!

We have looked at Jesus' teaching on prayer and in the next lesson, we will look at Jesus' teaching on abiding through prayer! But first, let's look at how to have a Quiet Time. This could be the most important habit that you establish in your life!

How to Have a Daily Quiet Time!

The busier you are, the more you need a special time set apart for building your relationship with God stronger. Most of us desire to be closer to God, but we are distracted with the tyranny of the urgent: bills to pay, diapers to change, or deadlines to meet. We put our relationship with God on hold, letting it slowly move backward instead of forward.

Desire! Discipline! Delight!

All we need to get started is the desire to get closer to Jesus. Our desire can take action and become discipline. Our discipline can turn into delight. If you desire to grow closer to God, then set aside time to meet with him daily. Start small—ten minutes—and build as time goes by. Better to faithfully meet with God ten minutes a day, then for an hour once a month. At first, it will be hard to be faithful, but **persevere!** Soon it will be a discipline. The discipline of prayer, worship, and Bible study is the best investment you will ever make—the dividends are wonderful! The fruit will appear—blessings, miracles, changes in your character and answered prayers. Best of all, you will get closer to your Heavenly Father. Delight will come in at the point and your quiet time will become the highlight of your day.

Set Aside a Time

A young mother needs this time more than anyone and yet has the hardest time finding it. If you are a young mom, keep trying! It will be worth the effort. Maybe your husband can watch the baby in the evenings while you have a Quiet Time. It seemed that no matter how early I arose, the minute my children heard me move, they were wide awake! So I learned to lie perfectly still and pray in bed before rising. I still do it because it's such a habit. Then I laugh at myself because I can have a Quiet Time easily now. I would read the Bible while I was nursing or when the babies went down for naps after lunch. It wasn't ideal, having to split prayer and Bible reading, but it worked for me for years. When I couldn't get time alone to read the Bible, I would simply read it aloud to my children. I added expression and used different voices. My children were delighted!

"Be still, and know that I am God" (Psalm 46:10 NIV ©1973).

Set Aside a Place

Find a place where you can quiet your heart and mind. Often, this will require a quiet place. In my house, trying to find quiet is hard—you have to hide somewhere with a door closed. Our minds are often racing in a million different directions, so we may need a few minutes to calm down and focus on Jesus.

My friend, Bonnie, has an actual prayer closet in a closet. She has to go into the closet to pray or she sees all the things around her house that need to be done and she gets distracted. I enjoy my beautiful bed—my husband made me a headboard that has a lattice arch covered with silk flowers, so I feel like I'm in a garden. Sometimes when I pray, I walk through my neighborhood. I try to find a time where people are not around—early in the morning on weekends or right after the school bus leaves on weekdays. If you ever see an older woman with long blonde hair wandering around Lake Mary, talking to herself, and possibly motioning with her hands, that's me! I'm really praying to the Lord! When I pray in my bedroom, I pace. There are tread marks in my carpet. The motion of walking keeps me from being distracted. When I am kneeling, I can start thinking about other things.

You will discover what time and place work best for you.

Set Aside Time to Thank God for His Blessings

In Psalm 100:4, we are told to enter His gate with gratitude. You see, thanking God will often fill our hearts with joy and praise. When we count our blessings, we are amazed by how kind God is to His people. Start your quiet times giving thanks to God. You might have to praise Him for the same things over and over until you learn to see all His wonderful blessings. If you can see, hear, touch, smell, think, feel, run, walk, dance, clap, or stand, then thank the Lord! Do you have a shelter from storms, food to eat, friends, family or a job? Count your blessings. Does your life have purpose, do people greet you by name, and can you find help when you need it? Can you read and write? Does your life have enough difficulties to make you run to God in prayer and long for Heaven? You are blessed! Be grateful for all He does. When He answers a prayer, make it a goal to thank Him for the answer twenty-seven times, not just once.

In my sophomore year of college, my roommate and I made a large "Answered Prayer" poster and hung it on the back of the door. Every time one of our prayers was answered, we wrote down the answer on the poster in different colors of magic marker. It was bright and colorful. Our faith grew with every addition we made. What surprised me, though, was how many people, once they knew of its existence, would look at it to see what the latest addition was—even non-Christians. We are created to appreciate and thank our God. We are energized when we see the power of God at work through answered prayer!

Set Aside Time to Worship God

Worship is the act of giving a gift to God. Often in worship, we sing Him a song, give our tithes, or surrender our life. Worship always involves a gift from you to God.

When you sing the Lord a song, make it a gift from you to Him. If you play an instrument, you can bring it into your Quiet Time, playing Him a song. You can sing along with a CD or open up a dusty old hymnbook. You can open your mouth and sing Him a brand new song.

Why does worship so often involve singing? It doesn't have to, but the reason we so often sing is that singing allows us to express emotion that speaking does not. The expression "he burst into song" is an accurate one. When emotion toward God overwhelms us, we "burst into song" to worship Him.

Set Aside Time to Repent

We often "sugar-coat" sin in our culture. In fact, no one wants to take responsibility for their own sin. It is always someone else's fault. We take pills and see psychiatrists to deal with guilt. We feel guilt because **we Are guilty**! Guilt has a cure. If you are guilty of something—**repent**! Tell God that you are very sorry and receive His forgiveness.

Make sure that you repent every single day in your Quiet Time!

"If we confess our sins, he is faithful and just and will forgive us our sins and purify us from all unrighteousness" (1 John 1:9 NIV ©1973).

Set Aside Time to Read the Word

The Holy Spirit, given to every believer, illuminates the Word of God to our minds. He helps us to understand the Scriptures and instructs us in applying them to our lives.

Always pray before you read the Bible, asking the Holy Spirit to teach and counsel you from God's Word. Reading the Bible every day is like going on a treasure hunt—there is always something new to discover, a beautiful promise to claim, or a principle to apply to a situation in your life. His Word is packed with wisdom. Be ready to experience change in ways you never dreamed possible!

God's Word is compared to spiritual milk in I Peter 2:1-2. When we regularly digest the Word of God, we grow up in our salvation. You will be amazed at how much you learn after years of reading the Scriptures on a daily basis. Truth will increase your faith, make trials easier to endure, and reveal the will of God for your life! You will never be the same!

Set Aside Time to Pray!

Prayer is our daily conversation with God.   Without
communication, a relationship dies. Without   prayer,   our
relationship with Jesus withers. We can pray all day long, keeping
the conversation going while we wash dishes, drive our cars, or go
shopping. This set-apart time for prayer is priceless. Here we can
lay all of our worries and cares at His feet. We can pray for our
character and walk with the Lord, while praying for others too.

We can also take time to be still before the Lord and wait. Be still
and listen for the voice of God. Let conversation be two-sided.
Don't just pray; wait for Him to speak to your heart.

"An 86-year-old, saintly woman approached me several years ago
after a conference I had done on time. On a crumbled piece of
paper she had written, 'Make sure of your relationship with God
when you are young and full of busyness because the time will
come when all the busyness will be over and God is your only
companion—you will not be lonely.' She knew how quickly time
passes and how important it is to establish a relationship with God
early in life" (Elise Arndt, *A Mother's Time* page 105, Victor Books;
1989).

The years fly by! Soon we will see Jesus face to face! Get to know
your Savior here and now. Face everything in life with confidence
because your faith in Jesus is strong. Quiet Times will strengthen
your faith, bringing you to maturity. Treasure your Quiet Time, a
place and time set apart for your **Beloved.** A place and time set
apart to grow closer to the ONE who loves you more than anyone
else ever will.

4 ABIDING IN PRAYER

Now we are talking about the abiding life with Jesus and how prayer fits into the picture. We had a wonderful look at prayer through Luke 11—what a great passage!

We are going to look at John 15 again. Let's quickly review what we mentioned two weeks ago. There are three roles mentioned in this chapter: branch, vine, and gardener. The gardener in our lives is God the Father, caring for and looking for good fruit. Jesus is the Vine, the source of all we need for life and fruit production. We are branches. Our purpose is to bear fruit, but our responsibility is to abide. We cannot bear fruit apart from abiding in the Vine.

Read John 15:1-8

Why are clean?

What is Jesus referring to when He talks about us being "clean"?

What can we accomplish apart from The Vine, Jesus?

Remember that the fruit that God is looking for in our lives is the fruit of the Spirit, mentioned in Galatians 5:22-23: love, joy, peace, patience, kindness, goodness, gentleness, faithfulness, and self-control. God is looking for us **to be**, rather than to do! We cannot bear fruit unless we are connected to The Vine, Jesus.

How does the Word keep us clean?

What role does this righteousness from God play in our prayer life?

If you _____ in Me and My _____ _____ in you, then you can _____ _____ and it will be done for you" —Jesus (John 15:7)

Answered prayer gives God **glory** and produces more **fruit** in our lives.

If Scripture is abiding in us (through hearing, reading, study, memorization, and meditation), how will this affect the prayers that we pray?

How can we abide in Jesus through prayer?

How does God prune our hearts and lives through prayer?

John 15:9-17

Remember that the Father's business is about making disciples, building His church, and allowing His love to transform lives. As friends of God, this is our business too. If, like Jesus, this is the focus of our life, then how will our prayer life reflect this?

Clean for Prayer

Only those who are perfectly holy God. We would instantly be the righteousness of Christ that to the Father. We are clean pure can approach a burned up if not for allows us free access because of the blood of Jesus, His sacrifice on the cross, and the Word of God. You and I can approach the Throne of Grace and receive comfort in our time of need. We can pour our hearts out to our Heavenly Father and He will listen to us pray! More than that, He will answer.

We don't have to pray loud enough for God to hear us. His ear is inclined toward His children's cries. He is delighted to hear us pray to Him and eager to give us good gifts.

Abiding prayer begins with the Word of God dwelling in our hearts. The more we know and obey the Bible, the more we will pray according to the will of God. We will have the same desires in our hearts that God has on His heart. Jesus can deposit prayers in our hearts.

God will even prune through our prayers. As we pray for things that are not the best for us, the Lord changes our hearts over time—soon our prayers change. We can also pray for freedom in our life as we find things in God's Mirror that should be changed. We can pray for transformation. God will prune/change us in answer to our prayers. Remember the purpose of pruning is to make you more fruitful—full of love, joy, peace, patience, kindness, goodness, faithfulness, gentleness, and self-control.

We have already talked about how God's business is to make disciples, build His church, and transform lives with His love. This business shows up in our prayer life. We pray about the things that are important to our Heavenly Father. His agenda becomes our agenda. Our prayer life is evidence of our passion for the Father's business.

Connected in Prayer

Abiding in prayer means to pray God's will throughout the day. There is our prayer time in our Quiet Times and then there is that abiding prayer that takes place 24/7. This prayer is like breathing. We speak to God and listen to hear His voice. It is conversational prayer, building our relationship with Jesus stronger and stronger. His Word directs our prayers by transforming our hearts so that we desire His will.

Abiding through prayer connects us to the Vine. We are connected to Jesus through prayer when we pray continually throughout our day. We keep our eyes on Jesus and think about Him as we make decisions, face difficulties, or enjoy our family.

Prayer is a command, process, and an act of surrender. We are commanded to pray, so we pray. However, prayer is also a process because the more we pray, the more we see God moving to answer our prayers, thus increasing our faith. This makes us want to pray even more! Apart from Jesus, we can do nothing. Prayer is a way that we can stay connected and grow closer to Him. In prayer, we surrender all that we are to Him, to His will and plan for our lives.

Love and prayer are connected through abiding! If we love God, we will obey Him and pray! As we pray, God answers which results in GLORY for Himself and more FRUIT in our lives! A win-win situation if I ever saw one!

The Adventure of Abiding Prayer

When the Word of God in lives inside of you, the enemy is unable to deceive you because you know the Truth. The enemy tricks us and tries to discourage or distract us from praying. We focus on all the prayers we are still waiting on answers to, instead of thanking God for all that He has already done. Thankfulness will build faith during prayer. We also get distracted by voices, noises, television, things that need to be done, or worries about our life. If something comes to your mind during prayer time, just quickly pray about it and then go back to whatever you were praying for before you got distracted.

The Word of God helps us to be skilled at discerning the will of God. We need to be able to discern His will from the enemy's deceptions. We must be humble when we think something is God's will and be willing to be wrong. All Christians miss God—otherwise there would only be one Christian denomination in the earth. Stay humble and keep praying. Allow God to direct and change your prayers. Trust Him when He says no.

"Pray without ceasing." Never stop praying. Pray while you drive down the road. Pray while you walk to your seat at church. Pray while you work. Pray while you nurse the baby or homeschool your children. Pray while you go to reach out to somebody. Pray 24/7—never stopping. Listen for the voice of God and keep praying, even when it feels like He is far away. He is close to you whether you "feel" Him or not. Don't live the Christian life by feelings, but faith in His Word and finished work on the cross.

Our prayer life is going to become more and more about the Father's business and less and less about our own agenda because we are abiding. The Lord will put it on your heart to pray for things because He can trust you. You will find yourself praying for people you hardly know—intensely at times. You will gasp in amazement when you find out **why** God had you praying for some of these people. Get ready for the adventure of abiding prayer! You will love it!

Prayer, that lovely communication with our Heavenly Father, ebbs and flows throughout the day, as we pour out worries, sing praises, and ask for wisdom in situations. He is always there, always listening. As women who abide, we must learn the art of "always being there...always listening." We can make it through difficult times because we are abiding in Him and He is abiding in us.

"I was immeasurable stronger than my usual self, and I knew it was because I was relying on utterly on my God. There was no way I could make it without Him. I knew it—and He knew it. Leaning on Him every moment, asking and receiving what He gave, I experienced His power and peace as a fruit of His Spirit in me. Such peace I could never have known if I had not abandoned myself to His care. He really does fill our storehouse with riches.

"But how important it is to ask—so that we might receive!" (Colleen Townsend Evans, *The Vine Life* pg. 91, Chosen Books (Word Books); 1980).

5 WALKING & DANCING WITH JESUS

The times I feel closest to Jesus are when I am filled with love for others, usually doing something kind, or when I am lost in wonder, worshipping Him. When we think about how **big** God is, how magnificent, how powerful, how wise and how wonderful He is— Wow! We are swept away into a place of longing to bring Him the honor He deserves. We want to bring Him gifts and to surrender our lives fully to His Lordship. Because we were created to worship God, we are at our happiest when we are praising His Name.

Read Psalm 100:1-5

Count how many times you see "happy words" (joy, gladness, joyful) in this short psalm.

What is the tone of this psalm?

Singing, shouting, worship, praise, and thanksgiving are commanded in this psalm. Why do these things please God so much?

We are called "His people" and "sheep of His pasture." Why does God refer to us in this way? Does this have anything to do with worship?

We are to enter His Presence with thanksgiving. When we thank God for all our blessings, His answers to prayer, His interventions in our life, and His gifts, we realize how kind the Lord is to us. Our hearts are filled with praise and, the first thing you know, we want to worship Jesus! That's why it's so important to start worship with thanking Him!

What are you thankful for?

What characteristics of God are mentioned in verse 5?

What are your favorite things about God?

Read Psalm 150:1-6

Who should praise God?

List all the different ways to praise God?

Which of these ways to worship are part of your worship experience?

I John 3:1-3

When does this passage say that we will be like Jesus?

The "gaze of worship" is when our focus is completely on Jesus while we are singing our songs of adoration to Him. We talk of "seeing Him." When we see Jesus face to face at the end of the age, we will be like Him for we shall see Him as He is. Now, we still see through a glass dimly, but in worship we "see" Him just a little bit. If this is true, what should happen during and right after worship?

The more we gaze at Jesus, the more we will become like Him. Worship transforms us, changes us, and inspires us to grow closer to our Lord and Savior.

Abiding through Worship

We abide through worship. As we exalt Jesus with our hearts, minds and words, His Spirit is free to be in charge. We surrender in worship, yielding to the leading and working of the Holy Spirit, whose job it is to conform us to the image of Christ.

What a glorious privilege to worship a Holy God! How amazing that we can come into His Presence and survive **His Holiness.** No longer required to sacrifice a lamb because of the Precious Lamb of God slain for our sins, we come boldly to the Majestic Throne of the Ancient of Days. What a joy!

As we gaze on the loveliness of the character of God, we are changed and our priorities are rearranged. As we fix our eyes on Jesus and all He has done out of love for us, we become more like the object of our affection.

In our normal daily lives, we walk with God by obeying Him, serving Him, and being led by His Spirit. In worship, we dance with God. We are free of earthly cares because our gaze is so completely fixed on Him. We are able to be lifted up on wings of Joy!

In our normal daily lives, we walk with God.

In worship, we dance with God.

The Way We Worship!

The Bible gives us guidelines for worship in the Psalms. We also have examples in the pages of Scripture of devoted men and women who worshipped God! Before Jesus came, the Jews, God's Chosen People, worshipped with dancing, singing, and giving tithes. Most importantly, they sacrificed burnt offerings to the Lord. Jesus was the final burnt offering. He was sacrificed once and for all. Now we have direct access to the Holy of Holies through His blood. Every time we worship, we remember what He accomplished for us on the cross—that's why so many worship songs mention the cross and the resurrection!

While Mike was in seminary, we had two small children, so getting off to church was an **event**. Often, we ended up snapping at one another and sometimes had full-blown arguments. How many times did I sing the first worship song during those years with anger in my heart toward my husband? But a funny thing would always happen. Before the first song was over, I would repent to the Lord for my anger and apologize to my husband!

We are transformed in worship. We often will repent for things we have done or said as we begin to honor the Lord and sing His praise.

Let's take a quick look at the different ways God commands and that people worship in Scripture!

Make Music with instruments to Praise the Lord! (Psalm 150)

Twirl and dance to Praise His Name! (Psalm 149:3)

Celebrate God's Abundant Goodness! (Psalm 145:7)

Sing brand new songs to the Lord. (Psalm 96:1)

Shout for Joy to the Lord! (Psalm 100:1)

Bow down, kneel in reverence to Worship the Lord. (Psalm 95:6)

Lift hands in praise to God. (Psalm 88:9 and Psalm 28:2)

If God commanded us to shout, sing, dance, and clap, He must like it. Often times, people talk about what they are comfortable with in worship—as if it's all about us! Hmmm....I think worship is all about God. So it really doesn't matter what we are comfortable with, what style of music we like, or how long we want it to last. What really matters is what Jesus wants from us. My prayer before I lead worship each week is that He will receive from us the worship and worshippers that He is seeking.

Tuesday mornings at 8:30, I attend a Christian spinning class. We exercise to Christian music and listen to encouraging words read aloud from the Bible and Christian authors. Often, I leave the class so encouraged that I burst into singing on my way to the car. As we encourage others, you'll know that you've been effective when they walk away singing.

One more thing about praise and worship...You often hear people talk about the difference between praise and worship. Most people think that praise songs are the fast, loud songs and worship songs are the quiet songs. Well, that's not quite right. Worship can get really loud. Praise can be gentle too. Though the words are used interchangeably, there are some distinctions.

Praise

Praise flows out of a thankful heart. It is directed to God or the people around you about God. (You can "praise someone to their parent or spouse.") Praise celebrates the goodness and mercy of God. It is often dynamic, vocal, energetic, and sometimes loud. Praise is all about who God is and what God's done! Praise can be accompanied with singing, shouting, proclaiming, dancing, musical instruments, warfare, and clapping.

Worship

Worship flows out of wonder and humility, ascribing worth and value to God. Worship **always** involves giving Jesus a gift. The gift could be financial (tithes, offering), physical (singing a song, writing a song, a dance, fasting food or water), or spiritual (surrender your heart, will, spirit to the Lord.) Worship is intimate and emotional, the unashamed act of pouring out our whole being to the One who made and loves us. Affection, devotion, wonder, stillness, holiness, communion, fellowship, intimacy, and dedication are also associated with worship. In worship, we are captivated by Jesus, finding ourselves gazing at His beauty, power and love until we **have to** give Him a **gift**!

10 Ways to Fill our Lives with Worship

1. Begin each day by counting your blessings.
2. Listen to worship CDs in the car.
3. Make up songs and sing them to Jesus.
4. Play an instrument and/or sing to the Lord in your Quiet Times.

5. Read five psalms every day in your Quiet Time. If you recognize a song or hymn in the psalm, then sing it! (Many hymns and psalms come from the book of psalms.)
6. When something good happens, tell people. It will fill your heart with gratitude. Gratitude leads to praise!
7. Get to church a little early and prepare your heart for worship. Be thinking about God before the first chord is played and the service begins.
8. Sing some songs as loud as you can while clapping. Sings other songs as quiet as possible with a gentle voice. As you choose which songs should be sung energetically and which should be sung softly, you will be thinking at a deeper level about the worship songs you sing. Next time you worship, put some thought into what you are actually singing and what type of worship it is.
9. Try kneeling or bowing down when you sing. Also try lifting your hands and expressing your heart through hand motions. If you know sign language, then sign a song to the Lord instead of singing it!
10. Get together with some worshippers. Turn off the lights and simply sing and worship.

Adding Worship to Your Quiet Time

By Laura Nolette

It was suggested that we add worship to our Quiet Times. One might ask, "Why should I add worship to my Quiet Time?" or even, "How would I add worship to my Quiet Times?" I propose that not only should you add it, but also that it is simple to add it.

To be successful at an endeavor, it helps to understand the value of it. Worship is a selfless act. It requires you to look outside yourself and focus on the greater value of another—namely God. Worship turns the heart, mind, and soul towards God. Worship focuses your adoration where it is due. Once time is spent worshiping, the heart is prepared to accept what God has to say, which is one of the main reasons for having a daily Quiet Time.

The technique for adding worship changes with a person's familiarity with worship and music. Anyone uncomfortable with playing an instrument need only to select and obtain recordings of two to four good worship songs they know and love. A good worship song is one whose words are based strongly on Scripture (or come directly from Scripture) and express adoration and/or thankfulness to Jesus and/or God.

Once you have obtained the songs and have put them, with a device for playing them, in your "prayer closet," you need only play at least two of them at the start of your next Quiet Time. Listen to the words. Feel the emotion of the music. Sing along with the words. Own them. Let these words be your own words. Express your emotions to God through the words of the songs.

Once you are comfortable with, or at least well practiced, in this technique, pull out your guitar or keyboard, if you play one of them. Instruments that prevent you from singing won't work for this. You don't have to be good; you need only know a handful (3-6) of chords. Rotate two or three chords while singing your own words of adoration.

If you feel incapable of coming up with your own words, sing a Psalm. If you don't play an instrument, sing your song or the psalm acappella (without instruments.) The melody isn't important, only the words are.

If these techniques are put into practice, your spiritual walk can be completely altered. You will find your Quiet Times more productive. You will also find that the worship songs stay with you all day and you will find yourself talking with God (praying) throughout the day. This continuous conversation is the kind of intimacy which God craves to have with each us.

6 ABIDING IN HIS SPIRIT

In this lesson, we are looking at the Holy Spirit's role in abiding. He is the life-giving sap that flows from the vine to the branches. If this sap flows unhindered, there will be bountiful fruit production.

Once again, let's review what we mentioned two weeks ago. There are three roles mentioned in this chapter: branch, vine, and gardener. The gardener in our lives is God the Father, caring for and looking for good fruit. Jesus is the Vine, the source of all we need for life and fruit production. We are branches. Our purpose is to bear fruit, but our responsibility is to abide. We cannot bear fruit apart from abiding in the Vine.

Read Galatians 5:13-26

What is the conflict within us?

_____ vs _____ .

_____ vs _____ .

When is the sinful nature gratified?

The sinful nature is not only gratified when we indulge it, giving in to lusts, cravings, or wrong desires. The sinful nature is also gratified when we live by "The Law" rather than grace.

Let's talk a little about the Galatian church, the recipients of the letter where this passage is found. The Galatians believed in Jesus and were saved by grace through faith—just like us! But a terrible thing happened! After being saved by grace, they went back to trying to earn God's favor by doing good works. They required circumcision and other things to make themselves "ceremonially clean." The Galatians didn't need to be using these things to please God because the blood of Jesus made them acceptable to God.

Just as we were saved by grace, we should live each day in the grace of God. We are **free**! We should not use our freedom to indulge the sinful nature, but rather should serve people out of love. The Law is not our master. Our fleshly desires are not in charge either.

The Holy Spirit is the One who should be in control of our lives. He can lead us in the perfect will of God.

Who is the Holy Spirit?

What is the "Fruit of the Spirit"?

Remember the Holy Spirit is not a "spirit-guide" or a genie at our command. The Holy Spirit is not under our control. The Holy Spirit is God Himself, the third person of the Trinity. The Holy Spirit hates what is evil and loves what is good. This is our only protection from veering to legalism (back to the Law) or veering the other way to indulgence (doing whatever our flesh wants to).

The Holy Spirit's job is to rule, reign, direct, and lead us in the way we should go. He is perfect for the job!

We talked about how the sinful nature is gratified. Now, look over this passage and explain how we can produce good fruit instead.

Remember our previous studies about abiding. We know that to bear fruit, we must abide. Now, in this passage, we clearly see the role of the Holy Spirit in abiding. He is the life-giving sap that flows from Vine to branch!

Abiding Requires the Holy Spirit

v. 16 Live by (in NIV) The Greek word used means "walk by" or "way of life."

v. 18 Led by (in NIV) The Greek word used means "controlled by, led by."

v. 25 Live by (in NIV) The Greek word used means "been made alive by."

v. 25 Keep in step with (in NIV) The Greek word means "walk by, way of life." (Same Greek word used in v.16)

God's Responsibility

What is God's Responsibility revealed in the following verses?

v. 16

_____ by the Holy Spirit.

v. 18

_____ by His Spirit.

Our Responsibility

What is our responsibility revealed in the following verses?

v. 16 and 25

_____ by the Holy Spirit.

v. 18

_____ by the His Spirit.

God's responsibility is to make us alive by the Holy Spirit (Galatians 5:25) which happens at regeneration, or rebirth. When we asked Jesus to forgive us and take control of our lives and chose to trust in His finished work on the cross, we crossed from death to life. Our eternal destination switched from hell to Heaven. We were adopted as sons and daughters. The Holy Spirit is our deposit, guaranteeing what is to come! (See Ephesians chapter one.) The Holy Spirit dwells within us, making us alive in Christ. We are alive, forgiven, and free at all times because of the Holy Spirit's presence in our lives. That's one of His jobs and He's very good at what He does.

It is also God's responsibility to lead us by His Holy Spirit. In John chapters fourteen and sixteen, Jesus explains the Holy Spirit and the role He will play in the disciples' lives. The Holy Spirit will counsel us and remind us of what we have learned from Jesus through the Word of God. The Holy Spirit will give us direction in our daily lives. Most of the time, the Holy Spirit will speak to our hearts using Scripture verses that we have memorized, which is why Bible memorization is so important.

Our responsibility is to walk by the Holy Spirit, daily surrendering to the will of God. We place our lives on the altar and allow Jesus to be Lord of all we are, have and do. He is the boss and we are His servants. The Holy Spirit helps us to apply the truths of God's Word to our lives so that our way of life is pleasing to God. We walk by the Holy Spirit in living a life that is completely submitted to the authority of Jesus Christ.

It is also our responsibility to follow the leading of the Holy Spirit. He leads and we follow. He directs and we follow directions. If He asks us to pray for someone, we stop and pray. If He asks us to write an encouraging note to our husband, we stop and write our sweetie a note. When we live with an ear out for God's voice, we have the joy of hearing Him speak. Hearing God starts in our prayer closets when we have our daily Quiet Times. Make it a practice to listen, quieting your heart before the Lord. When you think God is speaking to you, test it with Scripture, and then obey quickly. Remember, God will almost always speak through Scripture that you have already memorized.

What Scriptures do you have memorized?

Has the Lord ever brought them to mind in a critical situation or moment, using them to give you direction?   Explain.

The purpose of keeping in step with the Holy Spirit is to bear fruit in our lives. Walking with and listening to the Holy Spirit will allow us to stay connected to the True Vine, Jesus, and His character will become more and more evident in our lives. Just a reminder: abiding leads to fruit production. That fruit is love, joy, peace, patience, kindness, goodness, gentleness, faithfulness, and self-control.

Pre-Requisites to Bearing Fruit

1. Regeneration (Matthew 7:16-20)
2. Abiding (John 15:1-8)
3. Jesus' Word abiding in us and abiding in prayer (John 15:1-8)

4. Keeping in step with the Spirit (Galatians 5:22-25)

As Christians, we long for the Presence of God in our lives. As we draw closer to God through His Word, prayer, worship, and keeping in step with the Holy Spirit, our lives will be transformed. We will find ourselves at home in the Presence of God and filled with joy. It is at this place, where we are able to bring the Presence of God into our homes. We are filled with Jesus and then we ask Jesus to fill our homes!

Making ourselves at home in the Presence of God is not an eerie, mystical experience, but rather an experience that starts with, but goes beyond, the spiritual disciplines of the Christian life. We start with Bible reading, prayer, and worship. Then we go deeper! His arms are open wide, inviting you to experience more of His Presence in your life.

"Where is His Presence? I asked myself, knowing the answer. It's never 'out there somewhere.' It's an "in-us" presence. Jesus is within us. We are the temples where His Holy Spirit dwells. I'd known these things intellectually, but in these quiet weeks the words were filled with new significance. Jesus' words, 'Abide in Me, and I in you,' were not talking about two different things. Both phrases were talking about the same thing! We can't abide in Him unless He is already abiding in us! It is only the life of the Vine IN the branch that makes the branch able to do anything—even to abide" (Colleen Townsend Evans, The Vine Life pg. 63, Chosen Books; 1980).

"His purpose is NOT that you will do more FOR Him, but that you will choose to be more WITH Him. Only by abiding can you enjoy the most rewarding friendship with God and experience the greatest abundance for His glory. To abide means to remain, to stay closely connected, to settle in for the long term. With this picture Jesus is showing the disciples how an ongoing, vital connection with Him will directly determine the amount of His supernatural power at work in their lives" (Bruce Wilkinson, Secrets of the Vine pg. 96, Multnomah Publishers, Inc.; 2001).

7 HEAVEN, OUR REAL HOME

The next lessons will be a little different than Bible studies you have done in the past. They will require colored pencils and drawing. Now, don't worry, you don't have to be an artist. No one will see your artwork except for you and God (and anyone else you choose to show it to). There is a purpose to drawing—it has to do with creativity, imagination and color. The important thing will not be what ends up on paper, but what goes on in your imagination when you are drawing. Are you ready?

We are going to start with the book of Job. You know the story of Job. He is faithfully serving God, loving his family deeply, and enjoying God's abundant blessings of wealth and health. Satan asks God for permission to take away God's blessings and soon Job has lost everything except his wife, who encourages him to curse God and die. He is covered with painful sores, has buried all his children, lost everything he owns, and his friends explain that his calamity is the result of sin. His friends say things that are true, but also lack understanding of God's character and the nature of God's ways. After listening to their babbling long enough, finally in chapter 38, God speaks. He doesn't explain Himself or His actions, He simply points to things that He has made!

Read Job 38:1-11

What is God describing?

Read Job 38:31-33

What does God say about the constellations?

Have you ever been far away from city lights and enjoyed the stars? Describe what they are like?

Read Job 39:13-18

What did God NOT give to the ostrich?

How did God make the ostrich wonderful?

The stars and an ostrich...what about the rest of creation? Think about all that God has made.

List all the beautiful things God has made.

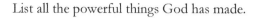

List all the powerful things God has made.

List all the amazing things God has made.

Do you own a passport? Have you ever traveled out of the country? What is the purpose of having a passport when you travel abroad?

Read Philippians 3:20-21

Where is our citizenship?

So, where is our real home?

If Heaven is our real home, then we are traveling on earth with a Heavenly passport.

I was born in Venezuela because my parents, American citizens, were working in Puerto Ordaz with US Steele, an American mining company. I was born an American citizen with a passport issued from the US Consulate. I was a citizen of the USA before I ever lived there.

In the same way, we are citizens of Heaven, even though we haven't gone home yet. One day, there will be a welcome home party in your honor. In the meantime, what do you know about your real home? Let's look at some passages in the book of

Revelation, a glimpse into Heaven!

Now, you need your colored pencils to draw.

Read and Draw from the following passages!

Read & Draw Revelation 4:1-6

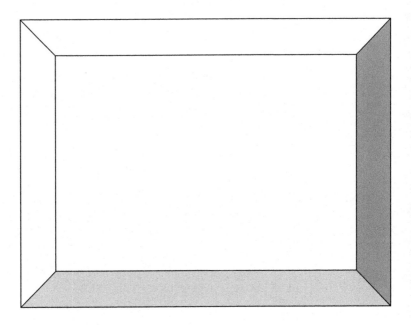

Read & Draw Revelation 7:9-10

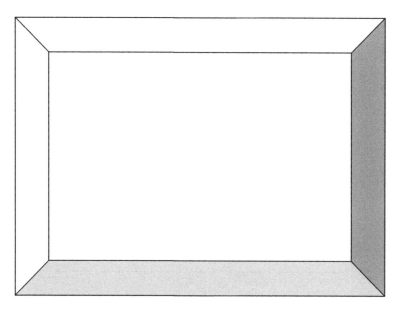

Read & Draw Revelation 21:1—22:5 Bride Beautifully Dressed for her Husband!

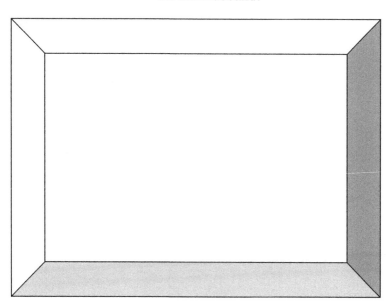

Read & Draw Revelation 21:1—22:5 Holy City, Jerusalem, coming down out of Heaven from God!

Foundations of City Walls

Light from God's Glory (21:23 & 22:5)

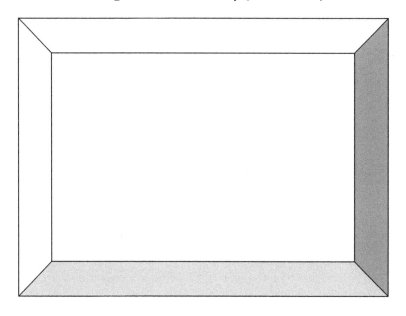

River of Life

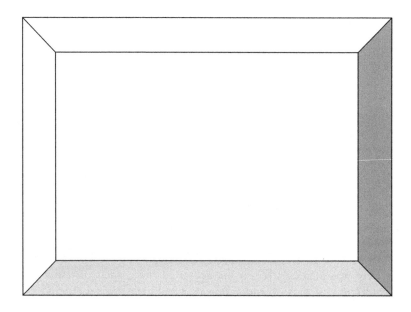

Did you feel inadequate to draw these glimpses of Heaven?

Why?

In these chapters, what things sound lovely to your mind's eye?

What kind of time and care has gone into the creation of Heaven?

Do you think you will like Heaven?

Why?

What do you most want to see?

Our citizenship is in Heaven! Like me, born in Venezuela with a US passport, we are citizens of a nation we have not been to yet, a nation that must be believed, before it can be seen.

The place that awaits us is lovely to behold, exquisite in every detail, and will capture our imaginations forever! God the Father, Son, and Holy Spirit, with great care, has prepared in careful detail a home for those of us who believe in the Messiah, Jesus Christ.

The Garden of Eden, mankind's first home, was filled with beauty. There was a tree of life in the center of the garden that was ripe with fruit for picking and eating year round. After sin entered the picture, we experienced the changing of seasons, including the death of winter, the fresh rebirth of spring, the growing season of summer, and the harvest season of autumn. Some warmer climates have two harvest seasons, but gone is the permanent harvest seen in the Garden of Eden.

The Tree of Life was central to the garden, so that Adam and Eve could feast, be nurtured and energized, living forever in the joy of His Presence. Heaven, like God's original home for Adam and Eve, is carefully prepared to nurture, energize, and give life to His people forever. We see a River of Life coming down, in the middle of the street, from the Throne of God. A river bringing life is again in the center of God's created place for His people. On the sides of this glorious river, we find trees bearing fruit twelve months a year. Not one or two seasons of harvest, but once again, permanent harvest for the people of God to feast, be nurtured, and live forever. The leaves of these trees bring healing for the nations (Revelation 22:2).

In every direction, Heaven is beautiful, filled with purity, joy and glory. In fact, no need for lamps, lanterns, candles, moons, or even a sun, because the glory of God lights up Heaven. How amazing! Not only dazzling beauty with angel choirs singing praises, but our very own Father, who has adopted us at such a great cost, is there. The Lamb is on the Throne! We are given crowns, but in His Presence, we are silenced in awe and lay our crowns at His feet. How thrilling it will be to see the Home God has prepared for us. Our tears will be wiped away and healing will come in fullness.

I Can Almost Touch the Morning

I can almost touch the morning
I can almost see the dawn
I can almost hear the singing
The sound of angels' songs
I can almost touch Your splendor
I can almost see Your face
I can almost hear the music
From that enchanting place

Meredith Curtis

And there You'll be
In the center of it all
My Holy God
Master; Lord of all!

Holy, Holy! Holy, Holy One!
We bow down and adore You
Glorious Risen Lamb!
Alleluia! Holy, Holy One!
We cast our crowns before You
Risen Son of God!

Receive now our treasure
We lay it at Your feet
Receive now this offering
Where grace and glory meet
I can almost touch the morning
I can almost see the dawn
I can almost hear the singing
The sound of angels' songs

Will it ever come
The day my dreams come true
I want time to hurry up
So I can be with You

(©2005 Meredith Curtis *Almost Touch the Morning*)

8 HOME, A REFLECTION OF HEAVEN: A PREPARED PLACE

Our Heavenly Father, with His heart overflowing with love, carefully planned and prepared a place for you and me. What tender care has been put into preparing us a home for eternity! As we gaze forward toward our heavenly home, we rejoice in the goodness of God! Filled with beauty, this nurturing atmosphere is perfect in every way. It is clean, ordered, and laid out in perfect precision. Nothing is missing.

Now we can imitate our Beloved King by preparing a place for our family, our friends, and ourselves. Our mission is to emulate our Heavenly Father in preparing our homes. With the same tender devotion and careful planning, we can create a place of beauty and order. Our homes can be a glimpse into Heaven for our families. Christian homes are a reflection of Heaven.

Marriage (a temporary relationship) is a picture of the church's relationship with Jesus (a permanent/forever relationship). (Ephesians 5:25-33, Revelation 21:2) Our marriage can be a picture to our children and others of how Jesus loves us and how we honor and love Him.

Our family (a temporary group) is a picture of the family of God (a permanent group). (Ephesians 2:19-22 and 3:14-15) As we love, honor, forgive and serve one another, we model what life in the Family of God (the church) should be—intimate, strongly committed with close ties that bind. We also need to be living this out in the church.

Our Home (a temporary dwelling) can be a small-scale model of our Eternal Home: Heaven. (A permanent /forever place). (Philippians 3:20) Our families, friends and guests can get an idea of what Heaven is like. Our home can be like Heaven on earth.

We cannot duplicate Heaven exactly, but we can follow God's blueprint and bring the Presence of God into our homes.

Read Proverbs 14:1

What kind of woman tears her house down?

Skim through Proverbs and list things that are considered foolish by the writer of Proverbs.

What kind of woman builds her house?

Skim through Proverbs and list things that are considered wise by the writer of Proverbs. (Especially see Proverbs 6:6, 10:19, 11:16, 12:25, 19:13, 21:9, 21:19, 25:24, 27:15 & 31:10-31)

Read Philippians 3:20-21

Where is our citizenship or real home located?

Read Revelation 21:1-10

Who lives in Heaven?

What does verse 3 say will happen to our tears?

In verse 4, what things will not be in Heaven?

What will life be like without those things?

Read Revelation 21 & 22

As you illustrated these passages, you were probably overwhelmed with the beauty of Heaven. Streets of gold and twelve gates, each made of a single pearl, capture our imaginations. High walls, made of jasper, sapphires, emeralds, topaz, amethysts, and other magnificent jewels, must reflect the brilliant glory of God with shimmers and sparkles.

The glory of God fills Heaven and lights it up so that there is no need of lamps, suns, or moons. The kings of the earth bring their splendor. I can only imagine that bounty coming from across the world as exotic animals, jewels, fruits, minerals, and inventions are brought for display in Heaven.

God's Presence is in the Heavenly City. He walks among His people, just as He did in the Garden of Eden. In fact, like the Garden of Eden, the Tree of Life will be on each side of the River of Life, available with twelve crops of fruit—always bearing fruit that brings life and whose leaves are for the healing of the nations.

Describe the atmosphere of Heaven.

What would it be like to live in such a beautiful place?

What would be the best thing about Heaven?

Read John 14:1-4

What promise does Jesus make to His disciples regarding our future home?

Read I Corinthians 14:33

God is a God of order and peace! What evidence do you see in the world that God is a God of order and peace?

Read Ephesians 5:1 & 2

How can we imitate God?

We can imitate Him in our home by ....

A life of love will prepare me to....

Read Titus 2:3-5

As women, our role in our homes is to be homemakers, managers of our home, keepers at home, or homebuilders. What responsibilities come with this role?

The foundation of our home is the Word of God and Jesus Himself. Nothing can take His place! We need to view our role in the home through new eyes. Just as God prepared Heaven for His beloved family, we have the opportunity to prepare our homes for our beloved families.

How to Prepare Your Home

1. Abide! Abide! Abide! (John 15)
2. Study What God's Word has to say about the home. (II Timothy 3:16-17)
3. Pray for Wisdom (James 1:5)
4. Be trained by older, godly homemakers (Titus 2:3-5; Proverbs 19:20)

5. Find out your husband's goals for the home and seek to serve him in those areas (Proverbs 31:11-12) If you are single, honor your father.
6. Be organized! Have a schedule! Have a plan! (Proverbs 19:14; Psalm 90:12)
7. Be a student—learn all you can. Keep a notebook, file, or other easy-access way to store information. I use file folders. (Proverbs 23:12)

We have talked about abiding in Jesus. Now it is time to bring the Presence of God into our homes. Before you begin, pray and ask the Lord for wisdom, study His Word and seek to imitate Him. Next, ask your husband if he has any dreams or goals for your home. Try to please your husband. Remember this is his castle. Make it a place he loves to come home to.

This week we are going to talk about preparation. We start with our goals and plans. Then we get down to business: organize, clear out clutter, make a schedule and get our finances under control. This is not a dream, but it will take time. Work on a little at a time until your home is a place of order and peace.

Goals, Based on Priorities, & Plans

Goals determine how we live. Even if we don't write them down, we all have goals in life. Sometimes we are not even aware of how big a part they play in our decision making. When I was a freshman in college, I began the personal tradition of writing down my goals. For almost thirty years, close to New Years Day, I review the year behind and look forward to the new. I pull out last year's goals and see if they were attained. After praying for wisdom, I carefully list my goals for the coming year.

Why don't you jot down goals that come to your mind? They might include an immaculate house or maybe just a clear path from front door to bedrooms. Your goal might be to have $5,000.00 in bank and be debt free.

Let me give you a guideline for your goals from the book of Matthew.

"Teacher, which is the greatest commandment in the Law? And He said to him, 'You shall love the Lord your God with all your heart, and with all your soul, and with all your mind.' This is the great and foremost. The second is like it, 'You shall love your neighbor as yourself.' On these two commandments depend the whole Law and the Prophets" (Matthew 22:36-40 NASB).

God's priorities for our life are: Loving God and Loving People. There is nothing more important.

I. Love God!

Worship, Prayer, Bible Reading & Study, Abiding, Holiness, Giving

II. Love People!

A. Marriage & Children.

B. Church family

C. Extended family.

D. The Lost (Evangelism/Missions).

III. Everything else

Goals are measurable and achievable! Goals are based on our priorities. We may say that God is our first priority, but if all our goals involve making money, then God really isn't our first priority. We may think that we really want our family to serve the Lord, but if a clean "showplace" is our highest goal, then we are deceiving ourselves.

We set Goals based on our priorities, so we need to discern eternal value.

Goals need to be measurable not abstract. Plans are based on goals. Here are some real life goals from real people. The plans and goals are achievable. They are practical.

Goal #1: I will grow closer to Jesus this year evidenced by greater freedom in worship, hunger for God's Word and overcoming stronghold of anger in my life.

Plan #1: Increase daily Quiet Times to 1 hour 30 min. with 30 min. devoted to singing and worship dance.

Plan #2: Complete intensive Bible study on book of Ephesians.

Plan #3: Memorize 4 verses on controlling anger.

Plan #4: Share anger problem with friend, have her pray for me and keep me accountable.

Goal #2: Our marriage will honor the Lord evidenced by kind communication and lack of arguments.

Plan #1: Read Marriage Builder together.

Plan #2: Bi-monthly date with only positive communication.

Plan #3: Memorize 3 Scriptures related to marriage.

Plan #4: Ask a godly couple to teach us how to work out conflict without arguing.

Goal #3: I will rebuild my relationship with my mom evidenced by mutual affection and time spent together without conflict.

Plan #1: Pray daily for healing of this relationship and ask God what steps I should take (asking forgiveness, etc.).

Plan #2: Break any generational sins or curses.

Plan #3: Spend small amounts of time with Mom that are stress-free on a regular basis.

Goal #4: My house will be a lighthouse evidenced by people in my neighborhood

Goals are about People, Not Just Tasks

Relationships are more important than tasks because people are eternal and lives are changed in the context of relationships. So examine your heart to make sure that your priorities are Biblical. Also, make sure your goals line up with reality. These goals should be attainable.

On the following pages, there are personal goal sheets and family goal sheets. When we think in terms of preparing a home, we need to think in terms of the family as a unit, rather than just ourselves. So, fill these goal sheets out and pray over them. The Lord can make goals happen and dreams come true.

Goals Bring Order & Continuity to People's Lives

"Think for a moment of the things God has surrounded us with—blue spruce trees, weeping willows by a lake, tiny paths under huge arches of entwined branches, ponds thick with water lilies, cascading waterfalls with spray catching the sunlight, geraniums red against thick green leaves, stretches of wheat and corn fields as far as the eye can see, orderly rows of vegetables bright in a spring rain, falling brown leaves forming a carpet underfoot, the first snowdrops bursting forth as the spring snow is melting, violets and moss at the edge of the woods, seeds spread out on your table which you can sow and visualize the growth ahead. God has surrounded us with 'things' which give continuity to life. We feel 'at home.' We can have emotions of satisfaction, quietness, familiarity, continuity, when we scuffle through the leaves at fifty-five in exactly the way we loved to do when we were five; or when we watch and count the waves breaking with every seventh one coming in with a greater splash—at seventy, just as we did when we were seven. God provides us in this life with a continuity in the universe which we may live with as we watch the Milky Way, as well as promising the wonder of all that is ahead for all eternity" (Edith Schaeffer, Hidden Art of Homemaking pg.80, Tyndale House Publishers; 1971).

Surround your family with order, purpose, and security by living a life that is proactive because that life is based on goals birthed from prayer and abiding in Jesus!

_____'s 20_____ Goals

Walk with the Lord:

_____

_____

_____

Marriage & Family:

_____

_____

_____

Making Disciples:

_____

_____

_____

In your Local Church (Personal Ministry):

_____

_____

_____

For your Local Church:

_____

_____

_____

Salvations/Winning the Lost:

_____

_____

_____

Dreams:

_____

_____

_____

Our Family's Relationship with God/Each Family Member's Relationship with God

Goal:

Plans to achieve goal!
1.

2.

3.

4.

Our Family's Relationship with Church Family

Goal:

Plans to achieve goal!
1.

2.

3.

4.

Our Family's Witness to the Lost

Goal:

Plans to achieve goal!
1.

2.

3.

4.

Our Family's Health and Education

Goal:

Plans to achieve goal!
1.

2.

3.

4.

Our Home/Running our Household Smoothly

Goal:

Plans to achieve goal!
1.

2.

3.

4.

Our Family's Ministry

Goal:

Plans to achieve goal!

1.

2.

3.

4.

Order Instead of Chaos

"A welcoming home has a sense of order about it. Not stiff, stultifying order that goes to pieces over a speck of dust or that sacrifices relationships in the interest of cleanliness, but a comforting, confident sense that life is under control. A sense that people, not possessions, are in charge of the household, that emotions are expressed but never used as weapons, that life is proceeding with a purpose and according to an overall plan" (Emilee Barnes, Spirit of Loveliness pg. 17, Harvest House Publishers; 1992).

Let's bring a sense of order into our home that permeates every nook and cranny. Plan and prepare so that life and stuff in our home is under control. There are several things that we can do to bring order to our homes. We can organize our stuff, schedule our time, manage our money, clean regularly, maintain our home, nurture our family, and fill our homes with joy.

Organize your Stuff

The basics of organization are to eliminate clutter and store things wisely. Each item you own should have its own storage place. That place should be practical. Things needed often should be easily accessible. Things that are used together should be stored together, or nearby.

There should be personality tests for your cleaning/organizing style. Just imagine the possibilities!

Mess, What Mess? Margo

Margo doesn't notice mess. She steps right over dirty laundry, trash on the floor, and every kind of clutter imaginable. Why should she make the bed, she's just going to mess it up again the next night. When mold grows on the tub, dishes pile up in the sink, or her husband complains, Margo cleans.

My friend, Laura, admits to not noticing mess. She can walk over a piece of trash and not stop to pick it up. Yet, she has learned to keep a clean house because her husband values it.

Pack Rat Paula

Paula saves everything, because you never know when you might need it. Her garage (or basement) looks like a warehouse. Plus, she is very sensitive and nostalgic—everything brings with it a memory that she wants to hold on to.

My Shine collects everything. She loves little containers and rapidly fills them. She is devastated when she has to throw anything away.

Project Patty

Project Patty might homeschool or teach Sunday school. She is basically neat, but she is always in the middle of one or more projects that produce massive amount of piles. There are stacks of papers everywhere!

This is me, with homeschooling, writing, worship songs, and correspondence, I cannot seem to eliminate piles of papers. There are millions of these piles in my house. When I get rid of one, ten more take its place.

Monk

You've seen the TV show! Monk is meticulous to a fault. Everything is clean, orderly and aseptic. You are afraid to touch anything for fear of contaminating it.

One of my childhood friends had a mother was a Monk. She had plastic covers on her living room furniture. Her home was beautiful, but not fun! Our mutual friends preferred our happily cluttered home to my friend's "designer showplace."

Balanced Betty

Betty's home is "mostly neat." If you watched the movie, *Princess Bride*, this is similar to "mostly dead." The house is a great balance of tidy and clean with "lived in" and comfortable. We all want to be Betty. My grandmother was a pack rat, but her home was always clean and tidy. She kept her "stuff" neat and out of sight in the basement.

The real fun in life comes when Margo, Patty or Paula marry Monk. Perhaps you already understand this dilemma too well. Whatever your struggle, work toward balance.

The War on Clutter!

As we seek to find that wonderful balance between tidy enough to provide security, yet relaxed enough to allow creativity, we ebb and flow from immaculate to chaotic. Remember, a home is a place for living.

If clutter has taken over your home, then take a deep breath and take control! Take one room at a time. Clean out drawers, closets, bookshelves, and cabinets. Throw away trash, give away junk or things you don't need any more, and put everything else away. Use shelves, containers, and file folders to store your possessions and paperwork.

I store all paperwork in file folders. Books, magazines, and photo albums are all on shelves. Everything else is in containers. Wrapping paper is stored in a large plastic rectangle under my bed, sewing notions are snuggled in roomy baskets, tea bags rest in apothecary jars, and hats wait in floral hat boxes until they are worn again. Craft supplies are in pretty tins that I can't bear to get rid of. (Where do you think Shine gets it?)

"Containers are wonderful! Just think, God chose to contain who we really are—our being and personality—in containers called our bodies. You may wish for a better wrapping, but what is in that container is the special person God made you. Your Creator has chosen to dwell in that container with you as well (Ephesians 3:17; Romans 8:11). Doesn't that make containers rather special?" (Marilyn Rockett, Homeschooling at the Speed of Life pg. 48, B & H Publishing; 2007)

Make sure that everything in your house has its own "place" and get everyone in the family, including you, to follow this rule: "If you get it out, put it away!" If you discover things that don't have their own place, then create one by emptying out a drawer or buying a storage container to keep it in. Eliminating clutter eliminates so much chaos. Peace and order will flood your home after you win the war on clutter.

Paperwork is my nemesis. Bills wait to be paid in a desktop divider, while letters nestle in a pretty basket. We store old bills in shoeboxes. All other papers go into files (or piles—smile!).

File folders are wonderful! Examples of file folders we have:

Merey's Personal Files

Encouraging notes
Housekeeping
Nutrition
Photography
Health
Traditions
Christmas
Ladies Ministry
Articles--finished
Article Ideas

Homeschooling Files

Math
Learning styles
Science
Health
Unit Study Ideas
Field trip Ideas
Books
Art/Artists

Household Files

Retirement Acct info
Bank Acct info
Deeds
Warranties
Instructions
Home Insurance
Health Insurance & Claims
Taxes 20—

Mike's Church Files

Bible Studies
Sermon Notes

Leadership Meetings
Discipleship
Brochure/Flyers
Special Events Info
Cell Leader Requirements & Training

Storage Tips!

- Store frequently used pots and pans near stove and sink
- Store coffee cups near the coffee pot
- Store glasses next to the refrigerator
- Store grains & baking products (grits, oatmeal, rice, sugars) in clear plastic containers
- Create "work centers" with things used together, stored together}
  {Sewing work center—material, notions, machine, patterns}
  {Scrapbooking work center—photos, books, scissors, paper, stickers}
- Hang dresses together, pants together, short-sleeved shirts together—makes finding clothing easier!
- Shake permanent press shirts and hang immediately to avoid ironing
- Fold clothing neatly and store neatly in drawers (you won't have to iron anything)
- Keep important papers in a fireproof box that is easy to grab in case of emergencies.
- When you reach forty and need reading glasses, store them everywhere. That way you'll always be able to find at least one pair!
- Sprinkle fresh whole cloves in kitchen and bathroom cabinets to avoid roaches!

Schedule your Time

At the age of twenty-four, the Lord blessed me with my first little angel. Katie Beth was born. After having worked two years as a nurse, I fulfilled my dream of being a full-time mommy. It was wonderful to be home with my precious little baby. However, I so struggled with time management. Mike would get home at 6 p.m. to find me still in my pajamas, not having even thought about dinner. Yet, I had stayed busy all day, caring for my little angel.

With each baby has come a better handle on time management. Maybe if I just have one more baby, the rest of the quirks will be taken care of too. When there is more to do and more little ones to care for, a mother is forced to become an effective time manager, or she must completely surrender her sanity. I recommend learning to manage your time.

Unless you want to fritter away the valuable gift of time, adapt a schedule!

Even if you are not a schedule person, use block scheduling and live by a "loose schedule" that is based on intervals, rather than precise periods of time. Before you put things down on paper, make a list of things you need to do on a month, weekly, and daily basis.

Once you realize what things need to be accomplished in a day, week or month, you can schedule them in. Dentist appointments, trips to the eye doctor, or the need for soccer cleats should not alter your schedule. These things can be fit into your regular routine.

Here is my list of daily, weekly and monthly tasks. There is room for you to make yours too!

Daily Tasks

Quiet Times	
Personal hygiene & Make Bed	
Exercise	
Meal Preparation	
Wash Dishes	
Straighten House	
Homeschool	
Return phone calls & Email	
Visit Daddy at Assisted Living	

Weekly Tasks

Laundry & Clean House	
Grocery Shop & Errands	
Home Administration	
Wash Hair	
Grade Homeschool Work	
Worship Practice	
Practice Piano & Singing	
Church & LIFE group	
Homeschool Co-op	
Writing	

Monthly Tasks

Color Hair	
Scrapbook/photographs	
Special projects	
Birthday gifts & cards	
Family Traditions	
Menu Planning	
Weed Flowerbed	
Bank, Doctor, Dentist, etc.	
Disciple Women's Group	
Health Appointments	
Take Dad to Doctor	
Homeschool planning & shopping	

Now that you have a handle on what needs to be done, pull out a blank weekly schedule and fill in the ideal schedule in pencil. Now, get real, and make your actual schedule. Don't be idealistic. Be realistic. Let your schedule be a helpful tool, not a slave driver. Our schedules are servants, not masters. Years ago, Laura typed up a schedule for me. I posted on my closet door. Still nursing Jimmy, I idealistically put 5 am as my "wake up to have my Quiet Time" time slot. Quickly, I realized my mistake and began getting out of bed at the more reasonable hour of 6 a.m. Laura, however, had my original schedule in her computer and called me early one morning at 5 a.m., assuming that I was awake. I was not and I am afraid that I highly disappointed her.

Make sure that you adapt your schedule to fit your needs, goals, and plans.

	Sunday	Monday	Tuesday	Wednesday	Thursday	Friday	Saturday
Early Morning	QT	QT	QT	QT	QT	QT	QT
Breakfast							
Morning							
Lunch							
Afternoon							
Dinner							
Evening							

Your schedule must accommodate all your responsibilities, leave room for the unexpected, and provide free time. Don't schedule in every minute of the day. Leave time to have fun,

Remember, our time belongs to the Lord. Honor Him with time. Once you make a commitment, keep it. Have a reputation for faithfulness. Your commitments need to be sensible, prudent and realistic. God can give wisdom so that no matter how busy your life is, you will experience God's grace. Think eternally, not tyranny of the urgent.

Before I got married, I was always early, unless, of course, I was on my way to class and passed of crowds of people I had to stop and talk to. This made me arrive slightly late to class. With marriage, Mike and I were mostly on time, though it was harder for both of us to be ready at the same time. When babies came, I became consistently tardy. Even when I was ready to walk out of the door early, there would be a sudden need for a diaper change, or the baby would spit up on me. It was so discouraging. I have worked hard over the years to be on time, but sometimes I still struggle. Motivated by the value of others and their time, I try very hard to show love by being on time or early.

Honor others by being on time. Give yourself room to relax and "prepare" as you arrive at various functions and give yourself room for unexpected (falls, bumps, dirty diapers, spankings, calls). Always have something to do with extra time if you get there early. If have nothing with you to do, you can always pray or worship. Aim for 15-30 minutes earlier than you need to be there. Often, we are unrealistic and try to cram too much into a day.

Manage your Money

Put God first in your finances, as well as in the rest of your life. Remember that He owns it all, including your money. As your family seeks the Kingdom of God first by tithing, avoiding debt, and living within a budget, God's will meet every financial need. Be generous to God and people.

Set up a practical budget and work hard to stay within it. God is the God of miracles and He can provide in ways that will thrill our souls! Pray first before you shop.

When we got married, Mike told me that we would never borrow money except to purchase a house and that we were too young and inexperienced to have a credit card (he was twenty-three and I was twenty-two). I thought he was crazy, but I submitted to him because he was head of the house. Everyone I knew had a credit card and borrowed money for everything, cars, computers, appliances, and vacations.

Twenty-five years later, after counseling many couples who were in debt, I am so thankful that Mike was so very wise. We only borrowed money twice—each time to buy a house. When we reached our mid-thirties, we got a credit card, which we pay off each month. Jesus has blessed me with a wise husband.

There is more information about managing your finances on our website, Joyful and Successful Homeschooling.

joyfulandsuccessfulhomeschooling.com/.
joyfulandsuccessfulhomeschooling.com/money.aspx

Live! Work! Thrive!

You prepare a home for people to live in. So, let the living begin! Open up your heart to view your family and yourself with fresh eyes. Everyone in your home is a beautiful and wonderful person, complete with his/her own set of talents, gifts, and idiosyncrasies. Maybe it's time to get to know each other all over again. Loving people is a great motivator to serve them by creating a home where they will thrive.

Live Life in your Home

Let life happen in your home. Make your plans and set up your home so that living can take place. Spend time at home—don't always be in a hurry to rush off somewhere else. Have fun together, make things together, do things together!

Do you know why television is so popular? Because we enjoy watching the action and relationships unfold on our TV screen, we become attached to the characters on a screen, rather than our own family and friends. They never leave the toothpaste cap off, have bags under their eyes, or leave something on the floor for you to trip on. They are **not** real. Your family is real. Turn off the TV and enjoy living with your family in your home.

Spirit-Controlled Expression of Emotions

Require peace and order in the emotional life of your family. Let communication in your home be positive and accepting. Every family member is valuable; no one else can take an individual's place. Pour out compliments and gratitude when it is warranted. People want their good deeds to be noticed. Lavish affection on your family and friends: hugs, kisses, loving touches, tender glances, and pats.

Anger can be expressed without causing damage to personhood or property. Conflict can be resolved with saying things that are regretted later, even years later. Forgiveness can be extended when we are wronged; grace extended when children are squirrelly. Get rid of sarcasm, negative humor, unwholesome talk, and any form of rude behavior. Teach your children manners and require them to be polite to you and one another. Use good manners yourself.

Work in your Home!

"It is not just aspects of your character, personality, attitude or spiritual state which will affect the lives of others working or living by your side. It is also your appearance and the way you care for the things in the bedroom, the bathroom and the kitchen!" (Edith Schaeffer, Hidden Art of Homemaking pg. 209. Tyndale House; 1971).

Taking care of a home and a family requires a lot of work. We are all different in our expectations and aspirations when it comes to who should do what. Whether you are a "Margo" or a "Monk," we all have to clean the house, do the laundry, and mow the lawn. Whether you are a beauty queen or "girl next door," you need to be fresh, clean, and attractive; as do the other members of your family.

Personal hygiene is necessary for health and self-image. It is nice to be around someone who has a pleasant smell. Teach children early to brush their teeth and hair, to bathe and wear fresh clothes, and to wash their hands at appropriate times. Everyone in the family can help- take care of babies and toddlers.

Large families create large messes, but the beauty of a large family is that they can become a cleaning machine. Our family is the Curtis Family Cleaning Machine on Saturday mornings when we clean together. There is something **almost** fun about cleaning together at the same time. A sense of camaraderie invades the home as each person does his/her job. A hardworking family can knock out the weekly cleaning (dusting, vacuuming, mopping, sweeping, bathroom scrubbing, and yard work) in two to three hours. The work is finished quickly. All that remains is periodic vacuuming, wiping down sinks, and daily straightening. Young children can help too. By the time a child is twelve, he/she should be able to help with all household chores.

2—4 Years Old Chores

Make bed

Clean room

Put toys away

Clear dishes from table

Carry piles of laundry for mom

Take the newspapers to the recycle bin

Water the garden

4—8 Years Old Chores

All of the above, and…..

Fix breakfast and lunches

Set & clear table

Feed pets

Dust

Vacuum

Sweep

Fold & put away own laundry

Straighten

Wipe down sinks

Unload silverware from dishwasher

8—12 Years Old Chores

All of the above, and ….

Wash dishes & clean kitchen

Take out the trash & garbage

Mop

Weed garden

Laundry

Clean bathrooms

Laundry is another **huge** chore for a large family. I wash between 15 and 25 loads of laundry a week. Different people handle laundry different ways. I prefer to do it all in a day and a half. I sort laundry early in the morning and begin washing and drying. The next evening, we all fold laundry while we watch a movie. It works for us. Other families do one or two loads every day. Whatever works for you, as long as clothes get clean.

Cultivate Joy!

Finally, cultivate joy in your home through careful preparation and spontaneous moments. Look at the bright side, enjoy these times together because life passes quickly. Soon it will be time to take our journey to our Heavenly Home and we will wonder where the years went. Make it your ambition to leave behind memories of laughter, love and joy. Let the Presence of God fill every nook and cranny of your heart and your home.

Remember when we talked about how the light of God's glory will fill Heaven so that no sun, no moon, no lamp and no other light will be needed to give illumination? God's glory lights up Heaven! Just as God's Presence affects the atmosphere of Heaven, let His Presence affect the atmosphere of your home. Abide in Jesus. Let Jesus fill you to overflowing. Then, allow His Presence in **you** to permeate your home.

Home Sweet Home

A Home is a....

Dwelling Place. Home is a place where you are comfortable, "feel at home," understood, appreciated, wanted, liked and loved. Home is where you feel safe and at ease from conflicts of the world. Home is a place to bring friends.

Prepared Place. A home is clean, orderly, and organized, requiring goals, plans, and a schedule. Goals for family members needs are met because plans are prayerfully made and carried through.

School: Home is a place where parents model maturity and teach/train children until they are mature in the following areas: daily life skills, walk with the Lord, character, emotional control, intellectual abilities, social graces, roles/responsibilities, interpersonal relationships, and development of gifts and abilities.

Nurturing Center. With a loving and caring atmosphere, home is a place where nutritious meals are served creatively. Dental care, good hygiene, well-made clothing, fresh air, exercise, Bible reading, prayer, and Family Devotions are provided for each household member.

Joyful Place. Home is filled with fun, laughter, joy, jokes, beauty, memories, traditions, hugs, kisses, cuddling, affirmation, music, singing, and surprises. Everyone loves celebrating God's goodness!

Hospital/Repair Shop. Home is a safe place where the sick receive tender care, broken things are fixed, broken hearts are mended, crushed spirits are refreshed, and the exhausted find rest.

Creative Productivity Center. Home is not just a family of consumers, but we producers who garden, bake, cook, woodwork, craft, sew, paint, paint, sing, play musical instruments, and write songs/poetry/ stories/books!

Hospitality Center. Home is a place where hospitality is practiced regularly and repetitively (Rom.12:13). Families open their hearts, lives, and home to honor and serve others. They link arms with their church family and reach out to the lost. Home is a place for showers, parties, game nights, dinners, brunches, and meetings for evenings, weekends, weeks, and months. Homes have guest rooms.

Ministry Center. Home is a place where the family give to the poor, serve the elderly, care for widows, minister to orphans, reach out to single parents, share the Gospel, mentor new believers, counsel, pray, bring healing, and host home groups.

Reflections of Eternity

Marriage (a temporary relationship) can be a picture of the church's relationship with Jesus (a permanent forever one). Ephesians 5:25-33, Revelation 21:2. Our marriage can be a picture to our children and others of how Jesus loves us and how we honor and love Him.

Our **family** (a temporary group) can be a picture of the Family of God (a permanent group). Ephesians 2:19-22 and 3:14-15. As we love, honor, forgive and serve one another, we model what life in the Family of God (the church) should be--intimate, strongly committed with close ties that bind! We also need to be living this out in the church.

Our **Home** (a temporary dwelling) can be a small-scale model of our Eternal Home: Heaven (a permanent forever place). Philippians 3:20. Our families, friends and guests can get an idea of what Heaven is like. Our home can be like Heaven on earth.

"Be imitators of God, therefore, as dearly loved children and live a life of love, just as Christ loved us and gave himself up for us as a fragrant offering and sacrifice to God." (Ephesians 5:1)

"In my Father's house are many rooms; if it were not so, I would have told you. I am going there to prepare a place for you." (John 14:2)

Let's imitate Jesus who prepare a place for us in Heaven. Let's prepare a home for others!

"The wise woman builds her house, but with her own hands the foolish one tears hers down" (Proverbs 14:1 NIV ©1973)

"By wisdom a house is built, and through understanding it is established; through knowledge its rooms are filled with rare and beautiful treasures" (Proverbs 24:3-4 NIV ©1973)

Heaven is Calling my Name

I Bow down at the feet of bronze
Glowing like a flame
I Bow down   at the feet of One
Who took away my shame
I lift my eyes to His, Blazing like fire
I see His face shining, Brilliance and power
Jesus, I'm reaching out to You
Jesus, You're making all things new

Heaven is calling my name
Heaven's declaring Your fame
Jesus the Lamb on the throne
You are the One calling me Home!
(©2005 Meredith Curtis)

9 HOW GOD DECORATES & HOW WE DECORATE

We read about and tried our best to illustrate the beauty of Heaven by drawing with colored pencils. How can we ever duplicate the beauty and glory of Heaven? Likewise, we can only imagine how lovely the Garden of Eden was, unmarred by the destruction of sin. However, we can see the Grand Canyon, the Rocky Mountains, Niagara Falls, and the Swiss Alps. The oceans waves crashing, the rose budding, the sun rising, and the eagle flying all call us to attention. They remind us their majesty of **One** who is more majestic that created them. Nature reveals both the character and power of our Eternal King. We also learn about God's decorating style, how His uses color, texture, line, form, and style. Before we look at Scripture, let's look at nature and learn more about the Lord.

List things in creation and "God's decorating style" that are revealed.

Creation	God's Decorating Style
Florida Beaches	Colors: blues, greens, neutrals Texture: sand, water, Style: Beachy! Cozy! Tone: Peaceful, relaxing

In Exodus 25, the Israelites are making The Tabernacle for the worship of God Almighty. The people are urged to bring offerings to the Lord for the building of this place of worship.

Read Exodus 25:1-9

Are there specific offerings that God is looking for, or will just "any old building materials" do?

What things are requested/required?

Who is the Tabernacle being made for?

Who gets it built to His specifications?

Who is our home being "made" for?

Who should we take into consideration when decorating and planning?

In verse 9, how is the Tabernacle to be built?

Why does God want it done **exactly** like the pattern He will show them?

Do you know what that pattern is?

What is it?

God planed and prepared the **original** Temple/Tabernacle according to precise specifications. The earthly Tabernacle and, later, the Temple were built according to that pattern. Let's look at how God wanted His House of Worship decorated. To learn the most about it, we will get out our colored pencils again and draw. Like the last lesson, you will get more out of this lesson by what goes on in your mind and heart as you plan the picture than the actual drawing. Don't skip this part. You will be amazed as God reveals Himself to be an Interior Decorator of amazing skill!

Exodus 25:10-22 The Ark of the Covenant

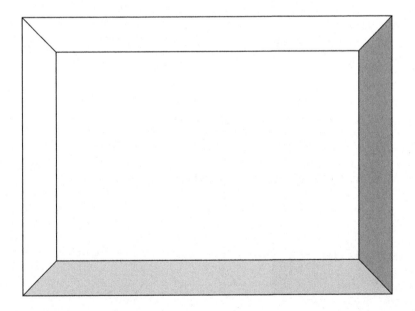

Exodus25:23-30 The Table

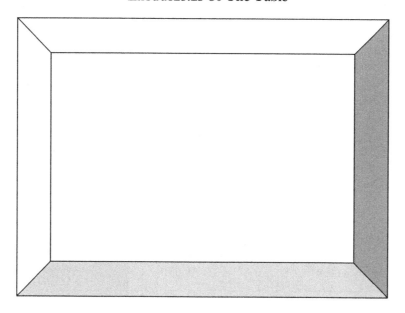

Exodus 25:31-40 The Lampstand

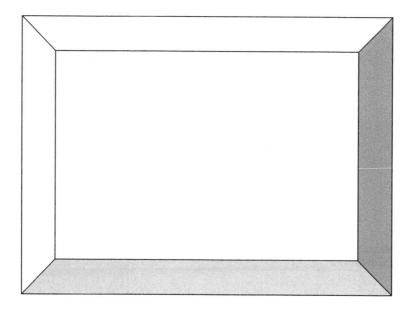

Exodus 26:1-37 Tabernacle Curtains

Exodus 27:1-8 The Altar

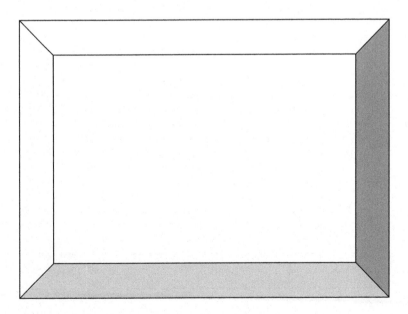

Exodus 27:9-19 The Courtyard

Exodus 27:20-21 Lamps burning with Olive Oil

Exodus 28:1-5 The Priestly Garments

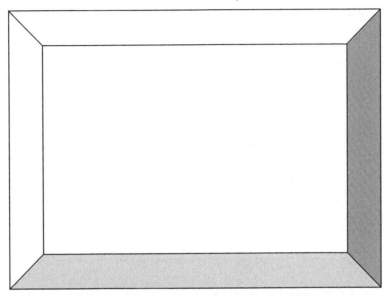

Exodus 28:6-14 The Ephod

Exodus 85:15-30 The Breastpiece

Exodus 28:31-43 Other Priestly Garments

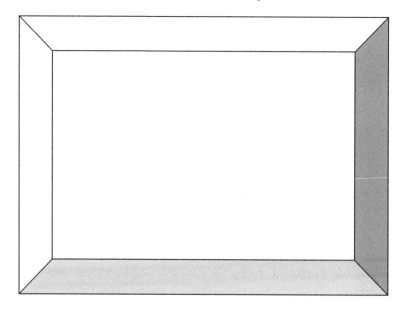

Write down some of your thoughts about God's decorating style, techniques, and use of color. Are there any items you see a lot of in His decorating? Why do you think that is? Let the Holy Spirit reveal things to you about God, the Decorator.

Decorating Like God Decorates

When I finished my own pictures of the Temple, I was not very impressed with my artwork. I was, however, humbled and amazed by the Artist who created art, by the Designer who created design, by the Builder who had His servants build a home for Himself that was exactly what He wanted.

Wishing I could see the Tabernacle and enjoy its beauty, I lay down that desire, knowing that I will see the **True Temple/Tabernacle** in Heaven, my Forever Home. There is inside of me, a desire to be just like God and create a home for my family that is beautiful and perfect for each one of us.

We are going to talk about interior decorating from a different perspective. Not only from a Christian viewpoint, but we are actively imitating our Heavenly Father, the Interior Decorator of Heaven. All of us live somewhere, and part of the "somewhere" is a place that belongs to us. It might be an entire home, a small apartment, our own room, or a corner of a room shared with someone else. That place is ours. We can begin in our own place to imitate the Great Artist who fills the earth and paints the skies with beauty!

"Surely each person who lives in an 'interior' of any sort should realize that 'Interior Decoration' is the first opportunity to bring forth 'Hidden Art,' in some small measure. And for the Christian who is consciously in communication with the Creator, surely his home should reflect something of the artistry, the beauty and order of the One whom he is representing, and in whose image he has been made!" (Edith Schaeffer, Hidden Art of Homemaking pg.66, Tyndale House Publishers; 1971).

Your Home is a Dwelling Place

Your "somewhere" is a dwelling place. The home you live in is a dwelling place. Just as we abide, or dwell, in Jesus, you live, or dwell, in your home. Beyond eating, sleeping, and cleaning our bodies, we laugh, create and make memories in that dwelling place we call home.

As we look at creating a home of beauty and loveliness, we must first remember the purpose of our homes—they are for living life—abundant life exploding with joy! Make a list of all the things you do in your home! Add some of the things you'd like to do in the future. In the past, we have gardened and canned fresh vegetables. In this season of my life, we are writing and recording music. A big difference, yet both involve creativity and nurture! Homeschooling happens in our home and college students come over to study.

Naturally, then, our home is filled with books and places to read and write comfortably. This is what I keep in mind when I decorate my home.

What happens in your home?

1.

2.

3.

4.

5.

6.

7.

8.

9.

Look over this list again. We need to consider each of these things before we decorate.

A Refuge

Not only is a home for living in, but a home is a welcome refuge from the stressors and burdens of life. When we walk into our homes, we should feel a sense of relief. "I'm home," every family member should say when they enter the front door. You, your children, and your spouse should each have an "unwind" spot where they can kick off their shoes and just enjoy the feeling of "coming home."

Our homes provide safety from storms such as tornadoes, hurricanes, and blizzards, depending on where you reside. Making sure that our houses are secure and ready to provide needed shelter is part of preparing and "keeping" a home. We have lots of candles and hurricane lamps that provide beauty and ambiance, but when we were hit with Hurricane Charlie and Hurricane Frances in 2004, we lost electricity and these candles and lamps served their true purpose. They were part of our refuge from the storm.

A refuge nurtures the soul, as well as the physical body. A quiet place to read the Bible and pray, comfortable beds to sleep on, and beautiful music to listen to all provide refuge. Decorating with peaceful colors, Scripture on the walls, and classic literature available to read, helps to create an atmosphere that invite home inhabitants to rest and recover from weariness and stress.

"Besides, a refuge is not a hole where you disappear to eat and sleep and then emerge to go about the business of life. A welcoming home is where real life happens. It's where personalities are nurtured, where growth is stimulated, where people feel free not only to be themselves but also to develop their best

selves. That caring, nurturing quality—not the absence of noise or strife—is what makes a home a refuge" (Emilee Barnes, Spirit of Loveliness page 15-16, Harvest House Publishers; 1992).

One way to make our home a refuge is to include something for everyone in the way we decorate. Each person who dwells within the habitation can feel that they have a place that belongs to them alone.

What You Like/What Your Family Likes

Think about your family. What does each person in your family enjoying doing, watching, reading about, or being surrounded by? What are their favorite colors? Do they favor a particular decorating style? Are there things they don't like?

When Mike and I were first married, I decorated Country/Victorian (and still do!). I filled every square inch of wall space with quilts, pictures, and knick-knacks.

"I just would like to see the wall somewhere," he complained to me.

"Why?" I asked him, my feelings hurt. "Don't you love all the pictures and quilts? What could I get rid of?"

However, once I got over my hurt feelings, I realized that what I saw as warm and cozy, Mike saw as clutter. There was just too much visual stimulation for him! He didn't want it all taken down; he just wanted **less** stuff on the walls.

In decorating our family's home, I wanted him to feel happy and "at home" too. However, I still have two walls in the home schoolroom, where he seldom goes, that are covered with pictures—my "Family Pictures Wall." You can't even tell what color the wall is behind all the pictures. (And yes, I checked with him before I put them all up and he gave me a green light!)

Now, it's your turn. Think about your family's likes and dislikes (colors, style, hobbies, interests, comfort zone). Write them down.

Family Member's Name	Likes	Dislikes

What about you? What do you like? Think about that. We'll talk more about it under planning. For right now, get a hold of some decorating magazines, sale papers, or advertisements and a pair of scissors. Cut out pictures of rooms, furniture, color schemes, and accessories that appeal to you. Then go ahead and glue your very favorites on these pages. Save the rest in a folder.

Color Schemes I Like

Rooms, Furniture and Accessories I Like

Close your eyes and imagine your dream home. What is it that makes it so wonderful? Write it down here!

*"I would put under the heading of 'Interior Decoration' anything we do with the place where we are living for any length of time at all. Here, wherever it is, is **your** spot. This place should be expressing something of yourself. It should be communicating something of **you** to your visitors, but it should also satisfy something within you. You should **feel** 'at home' here, because you have made it home with something of yourself"* (Edith Schaeffer, Hidden Art of Homemaking pg. 66, Tyndale House Publishers; 1971).

When you decorate your home, **"You"** will pervade every nook and cranny.

Needs/Lifestyle/Health Considerations

Right now, we have a drum set and a keyboard in our living room. No, it's not a permanent thing, but we have to work around these musical instruments right now. Books, however, are a permanent part of our home. We are all book worms, in the middle of a novel, or inspirational book, or classic (or all three!). Bookshelves are a need in our home---plenty of them—strong and sturdy. We have a big family, so we need a large dining room table to sit around and eat together. My husband is a pastor and our philosophy of ministry is relational, which means lots of hospitality! Practically, that means we need plenty of places for people to sit comfortably.

What about you and your family? What kind of life are you living? How does that affect how you will decorate your home? What specific decorating needs do you have? What about health considerations. My father often has to use a wheelchair, so I'm considering getting wooden floors so that he can get around easier in our house. The carpet is hard to wheel over. Are there health considerations that you must consider when decorating your home?

Interior Decorating Basics

Everything you use to decorate your home should have a purpose, even if that purpose is simply to provide beauty. If you buy a chair for the living room, it should be sturdy and comfortable. Dishes and silverware should be dishwasher safe, table linens should be washable, and dressers should be strong and roomy. Furniture and accessories should be functional. Don't buy a dainty living room sofa if your home is filled with rough-and-tumble teenage boys.

Harmony & Unity

The key in decorating is a sense of harmony and unity in each room, as well as an overall sense of harmony for the entire house. This doesn't mean that you have to pigeon-hole yourself into a style. You can mix expensive pieces with garage sale bargains. Victorian lamps can sit on a sleek modern table. The important thing is the overall "feeling" of the room. Does it "feel" and "look" like it fits together? Consistent color schemes, styles, and textures can help create this harmony, but sometimes an eclectic mix of colors and styles will "just work!"

A Focal Point

Choose a focal point for each room. This is easy in some rooms and harder in others. A beautiful fireplace in the family room, or bed in the bedroom, can make natural focal points. The focal point in the dining room is most often the table! Do you have a lovely bay window? Let that be the focal point of the room. If there isn't a natural focal point in a room, you can create one. A beautiful painting, or a quilt, can be hung on the wall that you see as you enter the room. A large mirror hanging over a beautiful sofa can be your focal point in the living room. Once you have a focal point, center the decorating of the rest of the room around your focal point. Pick up the colors in a quilt or painting; match curtains to the bedspread, or place a basket of silk flowers on the mantle of the fireplace.

Color

Once you have a focal point, it's time to choose your color scheme. Let's use a color wheel to talk a little about the basics of color.

Colors come in hues such as purple, blue, green, red or yellow. All hues originate from the mixing of the primary colors (blue, yellow or red). "Tinting a color" means to lighten it with white. "Shading a color" means to darken the color with black or brown. The intensity of a color is its strength, or purity. To "mute a color" means to mix the color with its complement (the color across from it on the color wheel).

Using a color wheel can help in choosing color schemes for decorating your home. Let's cover a few more definitions before we talk about colors working together. We mentioned "tinting" (adding white to a color) and "shading" (adding brown or black to a color). The value of a color is the amount (or percentage) of white or black in a hue. Luminosity, or lightness, refers to the amount of light reflected from a hue. The more a hue is tinted (adding white to a color), the higher luminance a hue will have.

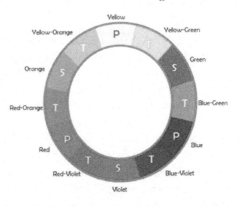

"Cool colors" are hues near blue: green, blue-greens, blue-purples, and purple. These colors reflect light and create a peaceful feeling when used in large amounts. White is a cool hue. When white is added to a color (tinting), it makes it "more cool." Smooth textures, such as porcelain or silk, seem cool.

"Warm colors" are the hues yellow, red, and all the hues in between these bright colors. Warm colors create energy and strength. Black and brown are warm colors and shading a color makes it seem warmer. Rough textures, such as burlap or stone, seem warm.

Color schemes that work together are adjacent, complementary, monochromatic, and split complementary.

Adjacent color schemes are simply two color schemes next to each other on the color wheel. Yellow and orange will create a bright sunny kitchen color scheme waking the family up at breakfast time each morning! Green and blue in a bedroom create a peaceful have to rest in.

Complementary color schemes are any two colors opposite each other on the color wheel. Red and green, familiar Christmas colors, are a beautiful combination of warm and cool. Blue and orange make a neat combination for a child's room.

A monochromatic color scheme contains only one color, but it is used in different intensities and values with a variety of textures that add interest to the chosen color. This color scheme can be breathtaking if done well. A variation of this color scheme is to chose one color, such as blue, and mix it with white, so that everything in the room is either blue or white. The same thing can be done with black.

The final, and most popular, color scheme, is split complementary color scheme. You choose one color, such as blue, and look across the color scheme, choosing the colors to the right and left of its complement. Blue's split complementary colors would be yellow-orange and red-orange.

Most often, people choose one color as the main color with two accent colors. This works beautifully!

Balance & Symmetry

There should be an overall sense of balance and symmetry in each room. If you are decorating with blue and white, you wouldn't put all the white things on one side of the room and all the blue things on the other. You also wouldn't put all the large pieces of furniture on one side of the room and all the small pieces on the other. Think in terms of balance. A short, fat piece of furniture can balance a tall thin piece of furniture.

Use windows as an opportunity for a room to breathe. Let the light pour in and dance around the room. Keep them clean so that you can enjoy the view outside!

Emphasize the Positive

Decorate your home so that the focus is on the positive. Camouflage the negative. An old couch can be covered with a pretty quilt. A scratched tabletop can be made lovely with a pretty linen cloth. Vertical lines add height and mirrors can create the illusion of a bigger room.

If a room is too big, make it seem cozier with large pieces of furniture, dark or warm colors, large patterns (on wallpaper or upholstery), and a dark ceiling.

To make a room seem larger, use smaller pieces of furniture, light and cool colors, small patterns, and white ceilings.

A Pattern & Plan!

Like all things, it is best to have a long-range plan or goal for decorating your home. If you know where you are eventually headed, you can take little steps until you finally reach your goal.

Figure Out what You Like & Need for Your Home

You have already imagined your dream house. Now, think through decorating your house in more detail. What do you like? What does your family like? What are your family's needs based on size, health, ages and interests? What are your storage needs?

What is your "decorating style?" Is it country, Victorian, contemporary, eccentric, artsy? It's okay if you don't have a "style," just figure out what you like and don't like.

Look at your house with new eyes. See your home in a new light. Walk through the front door as if you were a visitor. What do you see? What do you like? What would you like to change?

Are there any decorating problems in your home? Maybe you have stained carpeting, faded paint on the walls, or stains on the kitchen counter. Can they be fixed, replaced or camouflaged? A fresh coat of paint can make a world of difference in your house!

Keep a Notebook or File Folder of Ideas

Cut out magazine pictures or sketch your ideas. Store them in a folder or notebook that is easy to add to. If you find instructions for a project or pattern, put them in your notebook too. Make lists of things you want to make or buy. Pray over the list. Maybe the Lord will surprise you and give things to you so you don't even have to spend money.

Plan & Budget & Prioritize

Make a long-term plan for your home decorating—this way you will know immediately if your want Aunt Ethel's vanity or Uncle Jeff's roll top desk. After writing down all the things you want to do, prioritize your list. What needs to be done sooner rather than later? Which is more important to you, an orange tree in the back yard, or a new kitchen table? Pick one room or one project to start with. It may be as simple as painting a room or refinishing a dresser.

Don't assume that everything has to cost money. Trade things with friends, barter with your talents and watch God provide miraculously. Don't write off what you already have available to you. Search through your closets and storage places and pull out all the things you love. Now gather all the knick knacks, linens, baskets and lamps from the entire house and put them all together on the dining room table. Pray over everything and start over. Something that has been in your bedroom for years may bring beauty to your living room coffee table. See your "stuff" with fresh eyes.

Plan for Comfort

Start with sturdy and comfortable chairs and couches with smooth upholstery and soft cushions. Add blankets for snuggling under while you watch a movie. Spend a little extra and get good mattresses that provide restful sleep. Choose colors for the beauty and the mood they produce. Fill your home with good smells from cookies baking and candles burning. Delight the eye, ear, and heart with beautiful things to see and hear.

When people in your family are sick, bed-ridden or struggling against a disease, provide a healing environment with soft light, soothing music and quiet gentle smells. Lemon is a soothing smell. Speak in a gentle, soothing voice to your "patient" and keep the lights soft. Provide plenty of quiet and time to rest.

Fill Your Home with the God's Word & His Works

My first birthday as a married woman, my sister gave me a Proverbs 31 cross-stitch sampler that I have cherished for years. Verse by verse, this sampler inspires me to be a woman of noble character. It has hung on my wall for over twenty years. In my kitchen are two cross-stitch samples that I made on purpose. Each one has a Scripture verse (one on God's provision and the other on being content). Knowing that I would need to be reminded of these verses, I diligently worked on these projects and hung them on my wall. They remind me daily that "God will supply all your needs,"(Philippians 4:19) and that "I have learned the secret of contentment whatever the circumstances…"(Philippians 4:11).

The Israelites were commanded to take the commands from the Word of God and "write them on the doorframes of your houses and on your gates," (Deuteronomy 11:20) where they would be sure to see the writing and read it often. I have chosen to fill my home with Scripture on the walls where I can read it and be reminded that God's Word is true and Jesus keeps His promises!

Years later, when the Israelites crossed the Jordan River due to another miracle from God, He told them to keep memorial stones to remind their children what God had done for them.

"So Joshua called together the twelve men he had appointed from the Israelites, one from each tribe, and said to them, "Go over before the ark of the LORD your God into the middle of the Jordan. Each of you is to take up a stone on his shoulder, according to the number of the tribes of the Israelites, to serve as a sign among you. In the future, when your children ask you, 'What do these stones mean?' tell them that the flow of the Jordan was cut off before the ark of the covenant of the LORD. When it crossed the Jordan, the waters of the Jordan were cut off. These stones are to be a memorial to the people of Israel forever" (Joshua 4:4-7 NIV ©1973).

A friend of mine heard a sermon on this passage as a brand new Christian and started a memorial wall commemorating what God had done for and through Him. He framed pictures with his new church family, flyers of events he had planned, and certificates of classes completed. Every time he looked at his wall, he was grateful for all that God had done for him since his salvation!

Home Decorating for the Single Years!

Don't wait until you're married to decorate your home. You may not have a husband and children, but **you** need a home! You need a place that can nurture your body and soul.

"Single people in fact, may need to make a special effort to cultivate the welcome in their environment. If you live alone, it's easy to fall into the "hole" mentality—and deprive yourself of the spiritual and emotional benefits of a welcome home" (Emilee Barnes, Spirit of Loveliness page 16, Harvest House Publishers; 1992).

Don't fall into the rut of coming home, eating, showering and sleeping before you go back out into "real life," Make your home a home that you look forward to coming home to by providing things in your home that welcome you, refresh you and energize you.

"If you stop putting off "homemaking" until your hope of marriage develops into a reality, and start to develop an interesting home right now, it seems to me two things will happen: first, you will develop into the person you could be, as you surround yourself with things that express your own taste and ideas; and second, as you relax and become interested in areas of creativity, you will develop into a more interesting person to be with, and other people will very likely find that they will enjoy being with you more!" (Edith Schaeffer, Hidden Art of Homemaking page 66, Tyndale House Publishers; 1971).

10 HOME: A DWELLING PLACE & A NURTURING CENTER

We have the amazing privilege of creating a home for our family. Let's learn to make our home a dwelling center and a nurturing center.

Read Proverbs 14:1

A foolish woman tears her house down with nagging, laziness, gossip, slander, cruel words, lack of propriety, and lack of self-control.

A wise woman builds her house up with kindness, hard work, modesty, humility, trust in God, and self-control.

Read Proverbs 31:10-31

This woman has _____ character which is worth more than _____ because of her virtue, industriousness and care for her family.

A Dwelling Place is a place where life happens. It is a refuge, and a shelter.

A Nurturing Center is a place where the inhabitants are nurtured physically, spiritually, emotionally, and intellectually.

How does the lady in Proverbs 31 "build her house"?

How does she create a Dwelling Place?

How does she create a Nurturing Center?

In both a Dwelling Place and a Nurturing Center—real life happens!

A Dwelling Place

Remember when we read about Heaven? God's presence affects the atmosphere of Heaven. We affect the atmosphere of our homes. If we are abiding in Jesus and filled with the fruit of the Spirit, then our homes will be full of joy and peace. It will be a welcoming place to all who enter. Who we are will determine the atmosphere of our home. That is why abiding in Jesus in so important.

Read John 10:10

Jesus comes to bring us abundant life. What is your definition of abundant life?

What is your husband's definition of abundant life?

What are your children's definitions of abundant life?

How can we make our home a dwelling center?

A Nurturing Center

Read Psalm 23

What are the Shepherd's responsibilities?

How does He nurture the sheep?

Describe the table the Good Shepherd sets before His sheep.

This table is set before us in the presence of our enemies. God, the Good Shepherd, provides a bountiful feast even in the midst of trials, difficulties, and problem people in our life. The enemies are still there, but so is the feast. We can provide a shelter from the storms of life for our family. The problems and pressures may still be there, but inside the four walls of your home is a safe haven.

Here are some of the good things a shepherd provides for his sheep. How does God provide these things for you?

Green Pastures	Still Waters	Paths of Righteousness	Restoration Refreshment

How can you imitate God and provide these things for your family?

Green Pastures	Still Waters	Paths of Righteousness	Restoration Refreshment

Read Proverbs 24:3-6

How is a home built?

How is it established?

How are its rooms filled with rare and beautiful treasure?

List some ways you can build and establish your home. Also, list "treasures" you can fill your home with.

Built	Established	Filled with Rare and Beautiful Treasures

To Create a Nurturing Center

Nurture takes place in the context of relationship! Nurture is more than passing on information, it implies giving nourishment, sustaining life and imparting wisdom. We want our homes to nurture people physically, intellectually, emotionally, relationally, and spiritually. There are four ways to do this:

1. Being a source of nurture yourself.

2. Filling your home with things that will nurture.

3. Creating a nurturing environment.

4. Removing things that damage or destroy (prevent nurture).

Our Home: A Nurturing Center

Home is an ideal environment for people to grow and learn and become what God wants them to be. For a home to be a nurturing center, it first has to be a dwelling place where real people live real lives. It cannot be a group of strangers sharing food and facilities to "recharge" and then go back into the world to "really live life." A prerequisite to nurture is intimacy and real living. Communicating! Sharing! Celebrating! Working together! Playing together! Only as you really know others can you nurture them.

Physical Nurture

Sleep

- Comfortable beds
- Regular schedules
- Quiet during sleeping hours

Food

- Healthy (lots of whole grains, fresh fruits and veggies, and pure water)
- Wide variety

- Attractively served
- Mealtime schedules
- Positive conversations at mealtimes
- Special treats! (Make people's favorite foods!)

Exercise

- Model good habits
- Daily aerobic and stretching
- Active fun as a family (Hide-n-seek, playground, sports, walks, bike riding,   washing car)

Fresh Air

- Ventilate house
- Time outside everyday
- Avoid pollution and cigarette smoke (if possible)

Emotional/Relational Nurture

Acceptance

Communicate acceptance by:

- Listening attentively
- Speaking positively about household members to others

- Saying "I'm glad you're you and you're part of my life!"

Affection

- Hugs!
- Kisses!
- Cuddling!
- Snuggling in bed together!
- Back rubs (and foot rubs and head rubs)!
- Walking arm in arm or hand in hand!

Appreciation

- Always look for character traits to appreciate, behavior to reward, and things others do to thank them for. Most people feel that no one notices what they do. Be a "notice-er"!
- Use words ("thank you for doing that so cheerfully," "your artwork is   beautiful," or "I'm so glad we live together."
- Write notes
- Give small gifts

Loveliness

- Cultivate an appreciation for beauty, excellence, good music, fine arts, proper   etiquette, truth, softness, sweetness, and goodness.
- Fill your home with loveliness.
- Notice and appreciate loveliness, kindness, and noble deeds.
- Point out loveliness to others.
- Be quick to affirm efforts made by others to create beauty.

- Appreciate the artwork (people, nature) and character of the Lord Jesus.

Friendship

- Friendship enriches all relationships: our walk with Jesus, marriage, working relationships, family ties, and room-mates. We miss out on so much in our culture because there are so few intergenerational friendships. We can learn so much from those older and younger, as well as those in different life situations.
- Friends like each other! They spend time together, encourage each other, and enjoy getting to know each other. Friends have fun together! Let your home be a place of close friendships.
- Build friendships with household members.

- Model healthy friendships with other adults
- Build friendships family to family or household to household.
- Oversee children's friendships (cultivate good ones).

Kindness

Small acts of kindness are the sweetness of life. We are drawn to those who are kind to us. Unfortunately, often we can treat those outside our home with more kindness than those inside.

- Be gentle and kind.
- Require gentleness and kindness from your children.
- Appreciate all acts of kindness you observe in your home!

Godly Communication

- Let every word pass through these three gates before they are spoken: Is it true? Is it kind? Is it necessary?
- Learn to listen attentively and draw out their hearts.
- Avoid gossip and slander of any kind.
- Always believe the best.
- Ask gentle questions rather than accuse.

Handle Conflict Biblically

- Remove the plank in your own eye (Galatians 6:1 & James 5:19)
- Pray (Luke 6:37-42; Galatians 6:1-5; Ephesians 4:2 & 3)
- Look for underlying problem or need (Ephesians 6:10-18; Philippians 1:3-11)
- Confront lovingly asking questions, not accusing (first alone, then if needed, with a brother or sister, then if needed with the church (Philippians 2:3 & 4; I Thessalonians 5:14; I Timothy 5:9,10)
- Forgive (II Timothy 2:24 & 25 & 4:2; Matthew 18:15-17; Luke 17:3)

- Restore and reaffirm your love (Colossians 3:13; Ephesians 4:29-32; Luke 17:1-4; Mark 11:25, II Corinthians 2:6-11; James 5:16; I Peter 4:8)

Do NOT Allow These Things in Your Children:

- Bad attitudes
- Bickering, arguing
- Yelling, screaming, losing temper
- Disobedience (or delayed obedience)
- Laziness
- Sarcasm, cut-downs
- Complaining

Family Night

- Special dinner
- Family activity for all to enjoy
- Time to encourage and affirm one another
- Relax, laugh, joke
- Make up skits, songs, commercials, poems

Intellectual Nurture

Books

- Good books have high literary quality and high moral excellence.
- Let children see you read!
- Have children read aloud.
- Supply age appropriate, quality books in accessible places.
- Fill home with good books—classics, poetry, biographies, inspirational, historical fiction.
- Remove all degrading reading material.
- Family read aloud time every day.
- Discuss good books.
- Have children read aloud to you.

Conversation

- Raise the standard!
- Discuss good books, politics, history, ideas, God, the Bible.
- Avoid gossip, criticism and drivel.
- Ask questions.
- Listen to everyone's thoughts and ideas.
- Analyze news stories and historical events.
- Discuss application of Biblical principles.

Music

- Listen to good music and discuss why you like it.
- Read biographies of famous musicians, then listen to their works.
- Go to concerts.
- Learn to play an instrument.
- Sing together.
- Play music together, rehearse, and record.

Art

- Have prints/reproductions of famous paintings if possible.
- Discuss paintings and other works of art.
- Go to art museums.
- Look at art books.
- Provide art supplies: paints, clay, brushes, paper, scissors, glue, colored pencils, ink, etc.
- Learn to draw!
- Create art during family nights.

More

- Limit T.V.
- Maps, globes
- Computer games
- Board games (teach math!)

- Educational games
- Take apart old T.V.s, DVD players, computers

Spiritual Nurture

Bible!

- Read each day ALOUD!
- Write down Bible verses on index cards, decorate and put in a prominent place.
- Type up Scripture verses and/or passages on computer.
- Listen to Praise tapes that have Scripture verses or psalms set to music.
- Listen to Bible CDs.
- Read Bible to children with extra expression on your face and animation in your voice.
- Stash Bibles around the house--read when you can!
- Get away once a month for three hours to read the Bible and pray.
- Sing old hymns (they have lots of Scriptural content), psalms and praise songs.
- Focus on one verse or passage each week or each month. (Read aloud, Memorize part,   Write it down and decorate, Explain the verse to the children, ponder the words, their meaning, and application.)
- Start reading a passage. Ask the Holy Spirit to stop you at the verse He wants to teach   you about. When He stops you, use the verse to examine your heart and behavior. Pray for God's help to apply the verse to your life.

Prayer!

- Pray every morning before you get out of bed and every night before you go to sleep. "Good morning, Lord...." ".....Good night, Lord, I love you!"
- Pray aloud and walk around during quiet time if you get sleepy or distracted.

- Pray quick prayers for people or situations when they come to mind.
- Train yourself to stop and pray aloud when.....
    o You (or children) lose something.
    o You get lost.
    o You pass an accident
    o A child gets hurt
    o You begin to get angry or impatient.
- Pray in the Spirit throughout the day!
- Begin prayer by asking God to fill your heart with faith and guide your prayers.
- Pray with a prayer partner once a week.
- Journal prayers and highlight when God answers
- Make a praise poster of answered prayer.
- Pray prayers from the Bible. Personalize for self, others, church, nation.
  Ephesians 1:15-23, Philippians 1:9-11, Colossians 1:9-14, I Thessalonians 1:11-12, II Thessalonians 1:11-12 & 2:16-17, John 17, Matthew 6:9-13, Nehemiah 1:5-11, Ezra 9:6-15, I Chronicles 17:16-27, I Chronicles 29:10-19, II Chronicles 6:12-42 Philemon 4-7
- Pray Scripture for self, others, church, nation, circumstances.

Praise and Worship!

- Play praise and worship tapes in house.
- Listen to praise and worship tapes in the car.
- Read a psalm and sing songs to God in Quiet Times.
- Start Quiet time with thanksgiving (counting your blessings, thanking God for answered prayers, thanking God for circumstances, etc.)
- Worship together as a family.
- Make up your own worship songs.
- Sing old hymns.
- Make up new verse for old hymns.
- Make up new music for old hymns.

Family Devotions!

- Keep it simple, relaxed and short enough to maintain interest.
- Use devotional books or just read a passage aloud and discuss.
- Everyone choose one thing to pray for.
- Use illustrations, puppets, role-playing, flannel-graph boards, lapbooks if desired.
- Sing worship songs.

Discussions

- Talk about Jesus and His Word all the time!
- "What does the Bible say about this issue?"
- "What is Jesus teaching/speaking to you?"

Fellowship

- Encourage one another!
- Remind others of God's promises.
- Ask, "What is God teaching you?"
- Commend growth.

Evangelism

- Everyone should learn to share the Gospel clearly and concisely.
- Role-play sharing the Gospel and personal testimonies.

- Build relationships with non-Christians.
- Ask God for ideas to communicate His love to unbelievers.

Heroes

- Be a godly heroine!
- Commend godliness in others.
- Introduce household members to godly men and women worthy of imitating.

Transparency

- Be open and honest.
- Share what God is teaching you.
- Repent when needed and ask for forgiveness.
- Be real.
- It's OK to say "I don't know" and "I blew it."

Meredith Curtis

11 JESUS INVITES HIMSELF OVER

Do you remember that little song we sang in Sunday School growing up, *"Zaachaeus was a wee little man, and a wee little man was he…"*? Let's take a look at this "wee little man" who was willing to embarrass himself to get a look at Jesus.

Read Luke 19:1-10

What does Zacchaeus do to show that he is interested in Jesus?

How does Jesus extend grace to Zacchaeus?

How does this demonstrate Jesus' purpose to seek and save the lost?

Did the crowd seem to like Zaacheaus?

What do you think influenced their feelings?

Zacchaeus was a chief tax collector, so not only was he probably robbing the people in the city by overcharging them on their taxes, he was the boss of other hated men. Tax collectors were not popular! We don't really like the IRS today, but, for most of us, they are nameless, faceless people. In Jesus' day, the tax collectors salary was whatever money he took above the taxes due to Rome. So if Abe and Rachel had to pay twenty dollars to Rome, Zacchaeus could tack on ten more dollars. That extra ten dollars was his salary.

Risking his popularity with the crowd, Jesus invites himself to Zacchaeus' house for dinner. This invitation had a profound effect on Zacchaeus. He became more than a very interested bystander. Jesus wanted to come into his home and fellowship with him.

Besides feeding Jesus and his disciples, what else did Zacchaeus do?

How does this demonstrate repentance?

Jesus offered a spirit of welcome to this "wee little man" and his life was transformed. Even though Jesus was a recipient in this story, the spirit of welcome that should accompany hospitality was evident in Jesus' interaction with Zacchaeus.

Like Zacchaeus, we have invited Jesus into our homes. He is our welcomed guest! His Presence in our home changes us—we make adjustments, get rid of sin, and open our hearts for more of Jesus!

Jesus accepts our invitation and communes with us as an honored guest and dear Heavenly Father. Everything in our world is different because of Him! We are empowered and anointed by His Holy Spirit to make our home a 'Welcome Center' and a 'House of Blessing'.

Jesus has also issued us an invitation that we have accepted. He has invited us to live, to abide, to dwell, in Him. This abiding in Jesus brings rest from the struggle to work out our own salvation. We are clean, pure and forgiven because of His blood poured out on the cross. He welcomes us into His rest where His yoke is easy and His burden light. As we rest in Him, we are also set free from trying to impress anyone. We take off our "super-woman" masks, and humbly serve others, not looking for their approval, but seeking to see them grow closer to Jesus, the One we love.

Hospitality is the warm reception and generous treatment of guests or strangers. God says that when we show hospitality to strangers, we may be entertaining angels. (Hebrews 13:2)

A hostel is a refuge for travelers, overnight lodging at a reasonable price. Hostels are found throughout the world. Hospice is a ministry to the dying, where nurses and clergy provide care for terminally ill patients. A hospital is a place where sick people receive medical attention and nursing care.

What do all these things have to do with hospitality?

Well, I'm glad you asked.

Christian hospitality is a ministry that a Christian, or Christian family, provides to unbelievers who are dying in their sin, Christians who need refreshing, or leaders in the Kingdom of God who need a place to stay while they carry out their ministry. It is a requirement for elders to live a lifestyle of hospitality before they can be set in place for the ministry of leading a church. Hospitality matters to God. Why is hospitality so important to God that he commands it (Romans 12:13) and requires that it be done without grumbling (I Peter 4:9)? Hospitality requires love and serving in a deeper way than praying for Brother Joe, greeting Sister Sally, or giving money to the mission fund. Hospitality takes time, effort, and work. It reveals our hearts. Is there a spirit of welcome inside of us? Are we willing to let others into our world?

We can't fake hospitality for very long. If we don't have a spirit of welcome inside, we will eventually become weary and complain about opening our homes to other people. Regular hospitality also forces us into a situation of being transparent. Our homes reflect our ambitions, dreams, and hobbies. People see us for who we are, not the image we want to portray.

Hospitality does cause our furniture to wear out and our carpet to become stained. Is it worth the price? That depends on what is more valuable to you—people or things.

Our homes are a reflection of who we are. When we invite people into our homes, we invite them into our hearts! We spread our arms open and say, "Welcome to my world!" Hospitality blesses people! As we open our home, it becomes a "House of Blessing."

House of Blessing

A house of blessing, not only for guests, will refresh family members as well. Everyone should feel loved, welcomed, accepted. Let blessings overflow so that inhabitants and guests are lavished with kindness!

"We have wanted a home where guests feel like family, but family members feel like honored guests" (Emilee Barnes, *Welcome Home: Creating Your Own Place of Beauty and Love* pg. 8, Harvest House Publishers; 1997).

Humility

True hospitality is not about impressing guests. In a house of blessing, guests are welcomed because they are liked and wanted. Masks come off, and real people with real flaws interact with each other. There is love and acceptance flowing because Jesus accepts us, we accept one another.

Good Manners

"I grew up in the land of hospitality—the South. I'm now a grandmother, so I'm old enough to remember polite manners, good home-cooked food, Sunday dinner—that's lunch for those not raised in the South—starched linens and fine china on the table, and the family's best for company. Company came frequently and almost every woman knew how to entertain well" (Marilyn Rockett, *Homeschooling at the Speed of Life* pg. 146. B & H Publishing; 2007).

A lost art in our day, manners were invented to make people feel comfortable, so that there would be some agreed upon protocol that would enable people to know what to expect from one another. Nowadays, rudeness is the norm, not politeness. However, our Bible tells us that love "is not rude" (I Corinthians 13:5). Refresh your manners by reading a book on manners and putting it into practice.

What if you never learned polite protocol? Well, it is never too late.

Here are some basics for polite hospitality!

1. Welcome guests and say goodbye to guests with your full attention. All family members should stop what they are doing to greet guests, or say good-bye, at the door. Remember to always rise in the presence of older people; children should rise in the presence of adults.
2. Each family member should learn to make proper introductions and "small talk." Men are introduced to woman first ("Mary, this is John; John, this is Mary") and younger people to older (Aunt Betsy, this is Fred; Fred, this is my Aunt Bessie").
3. Offer guests something cold or hot to drink when they arrive, even if they're not visiting for a meal. Anyone who walks through your front door should be offered a drink.
4. Put your napkin in your lap and keep your elbows off the table.
5. Do not burp, or worse, at the table. If it sneaks out, quickly say, "Excuse me, please."

6. Unless it's a buffet, don't start eating until everyone has been served. The hostess should take the first bite, signaling that everyone else can begin eating.
7. If there's not enough food, family members should "hold back" without bringing any attention to the fact that they are doing so.
8. Learn the art of asking questions. Allow guests to talk about themselves or things that interest them. Stay attentive.

"People never visit Jenny's house without feeling loved and welcome. They never leave without feeling she's sorry to see them go. The first impressions and the last impressions in Jenny's home reflect her beautiful heart of hospitality. She says she learned it growing up, but I know she is constantly teaching me." (Emilee Barnes [about her daughter]*Welcome Home: Creating Your Own Place of Beauty and Love* pg. 31, Harvest House Publishers; 1997).

Create Memories & Reminisce

Think in terms of creating memories for you families in friends. Playing a game that everyone enjoys or serving a favorite dish will go a long way in honoring guest and creating memories. When you have known people a long time reminisce about things you have done together in the past. Shared memories cement relationships.

Laughter

"All the days of the oppressed are wretched, but the cheerful heart has a continual feast" (Proverbs 15:15 NIV ©1979).

The laughing family has a continual party! They live life with exploding joy! Life is lived to the fullest, every moment seen as a treasure to enjoy. This heritage is for all families who love and serve Jesus. We don't take ourselves too seriously, though we take serving Jesus very seriously. We can laugh at our mistakes because we have learned to be humble. We tell jokes and family stories that make us giggle. Sometimes we laugh so hard that we cannot catch our breath. Happy hearts make a happy home. Have fun with your family and have fun with your guests.

Appreciation

The secret of genuine contentment is thankfulness. Show appreciation to one another and your guests. Thank them for all the things they do for you and others. Be grateful for who God made them to be. There is nothing more wonderful than to have, what you do, noticed and appreciated!

My friend, Andrea, would make little gifts for her guests that they could take home. It might be a tea bag attached to a Bible verse card or a tiny booklet of poetry. This thoughtful gesture always made me feel welcome.

My friend, Mike, always shows up with a gift for the hostess when he is a guest. It might be a dessert from Publix, a game for the children, or flowers for the table. As a single guy, still living at home, he feels awkward inviting guests over, but he will invite himself over and bring the dinner! Pizza or subs are a real treat when you are a family on a tight budget. Mike doesn't let obstacles keep him from being hospitable.

Receive appreciation from those who experience your blessing. They will be grateful and want to bless you back. Don't say, "It was nothing." Instead say, "It was such fun to have you over!" or "It was my pleasure!"

A Home that Says "Welcome to my World!"

Your house can be a place that is a blessing to its inhabitants and visitors. Hang a pretty welcome wreath on your front door and put a pretty mat down for guests to wipe their feet. Or you could hang a welcome flag above the door. Keep the light on at night so that the doorway is highly visible. Keep your lawn and sidewalk attractive and well-maintained—it communicates that you care about things in your world.

Walk through the front door and look at your house through the eyes of a guest. When getting ready for company, make sure that the "welcome area" is tidy and welcoming. Fresh flowers and delicious smells from the kitchen always say, "Welcome to my world!" Let the welcome you feel in your heart come through your voice and nonverbal communication. Hugs and handshakes say "Welcome!" far better than words!

Display family photos so that people can meet your family, including extended family. I love to see a couple's wedding pictures displayed, especially if they've been married over twenty years. (*No, not because I want to make fun of their hairstyles!*)

Display gifts and cards that people give you so that they know how much you appreciate their thoughtfulness. The most welcoming thing in your home is YOU! So, dress attractively, smile and extend your heart!

Entertaining Angels!

We don't always know how much our hospitality will affect people. When my mother was planning my grandmother's 100th birthday party, a college friend of hers wrote a sweet letter thanking Beezie, my grandmother, for letting her stay in Puerto Ordaz with the family one summer. It turns out that her family was having problems and she was discouraged about life in general, and marriage in particular. When she saw the devotion between my grandparents and experienced their warm hospitality, it made her believe that God could have a good plan for her life. A summer of hospitality brought hope to a young woman! Fifty years later, she was still thankful!

Preparations

Often we turn hospitality into a chore and burden. We get it into our minds that everything has to be perfect. "Company's coming!" brings fear into the hearts of our children because they know that they will have to sweat and serve, making the house immaculate and listening to you scream and rant. Yikes! I don't think that God had that scenario in mind when he commanded us to "offer hospitality to one another without grumbling." (I Peter 4:19)

Our family is so big that we do not get invited over for dinner very often, so when we do, I'm just excited! I don't care how neat the house is or if the meal is perfect. I'm just so thankful to be invited to someone's home and enjoy their company. Relax. Your guests are there to see you, not your house.

Try to keep your house fairly tidy and clean each week on a scheduled day. That way when company comes, all you have to do is vacuum, wipe down sinks, and straighten surface clutter. Growing up, my mom would put piles of clutter into laundry baskets and hide them in her room. The place looked great for company, but we lost many things in the deep recesses of her laundry baskets filled with piles. It is better to keep the house **close** to being ready for company at all times.

If company is coming for dinner, set the table with extra care. Consider using **washable** cloth napkins on a pretty tablecloth. Add a festive centerpiece, if you don't already have one.

"Fresh flowers make a "wow" centerpiece, but an interesting one might be an unusual piece of pottery, or a Barbie in an eclectic outfit or a collection of autumn leaves or seashells. And add candles—not just for company. Kids love candlelight too. Making the table special adds to the appeal of eating together" (Mary Beth Lagerborg, Dwelling: Living Fully from the Space you Call Home pg. 67, Fleming H Revel/Baker Publishing Group; 2007).

Flexibility

Sometimes hospitality causes our physical dwelling and our family members to **shine**—look their very best. Other times, things just...well...things go wrong. I have caught the stove on fire more than once. A burnt smell coming from the kitchen never makes a guest feel very comfortable. Sometimes, a dish just doesn't turn out very well—even if it's something you've cooked many times before with success. Maybe you made your sweet and sour chicken, only to find out your guest is diabetic and can't eat your chicken, muffins, or dessert—all of which are loaded with sugar.

Just because things go wrong doesn't mean the overall time of hospitality can't be a success. If you are able, laugh about the stove catching on fire or the cat eating the pot roast. Dominos does deliver! Just think, you will have something to **reminisce** about in the future with your guests—if they ever come back (just kidding!). Laughter puts everything in perspective. Life is short and these little hospitality disasters are not worth getting upset over.

Sometimes your home itself may present problems. It may be too small to have many people over. Laura and Donald have a small home that is crowded when another family comes over for dinner. This doesn't stop them from having people over—they show hospitality all the time. They have learned to use their carport, as a covered porch, and their huge yard for hospitality. We have made more memories in their yard playing football, eating delicious grilled lemon chicken, and talking around a fire. We have watched movies with a big screen set up outside. In fact, they even let my son have his ninth birthday party with airsoft war games in their wonderful yard. A small house doesn't stop Laura and Donald from entertaining angels, and others too!

Opening Your Home for Hospitality!

Okay, you are convinced to open your home and have people over. Should you make a list and have everyone you know over one family at a time for dinner? Well, you could do that. That's what my friend Betty did. As soon as she joined our church, she began having each family in the church over one at a time. She is a delicious cook and people couldn't wait until it was their turn. (We do have a small church) There are many other ways to open your door and welcome people in. Here are just a few ideas:

Game Nights—invite people over for dessert and playing board games.

Card Party—set up card tables in various rooms and play bridge, hearts or spades.

BBQ—grill outside on the patio. Everyone brings a side dish.

Bible Study or Prayer Meeting—host one for the church.

Teen Night or Outreach Event—host one for the church.

Watch a Movie—invite everyone over to watch a movie. Serve popcorn and drinks.

Host an "After Church Meeting Fellowship"—let everyone crash at your house to talk, watch a movie, or play a game.

Open House—set a time of three to four hours. Serve finger food and punch, letting people drop by anytime during the "open house."

Supper Club—get together with two to three other couples and form a "supper club" where you rotate houses each week or month until everyone has served dinner to the "club."

Covered Dish Supper—everyone brings a dish to share. These are especially fun if there is a theme: Southwestern, Hawaiian, Italian, or International.

Tea Party—get out the fine china, linens, and white gloves.

Showers—host a wedding or baby shower.

Brunch—served brunch either sit down or buffet.

Celebrations!

Special events are more fun when celebrated with a party! You can have just your family, extended family and close friends only, or invite the whole world! Realize that the bigger the party, the more money you will have to spend on food and paper products. Don't hesitate to ask close friends to help out with bringing food.

Parties can be whatever you want them to be. Games can be played, a theme chosen and guests can even dress up in costumes. Or you can just sit around and talk. Parties do need food. Here are some recipes we love for our family celebrations.

Chicken Mandarin

Chicken Breast Tenders, uncooked

2 Cups Tomato Sauce

1 Cup Soy Sauce

1 Tbsp. Minced Garlic

Sage, Thyme, Cayenne Pepper, Paprika, Parsley, and Salt to Taste

Place chicken tenders in greased baking pan. Mix soy sauce, tomato sauce and minced garlic. Pour over chicken. Let stand for at least one hour. Bake 1 ½ hours at 350. After 1 ¼ hours, add can of mandarin oranges. Serve with rice. The tomato/orange marinade makes a good sauce for rice.

Lemon Pepper Chicken

8 Large Boneless Chicken Breasts

1 Large Can Cream of Chicken Soup

1 Cup Parmesan Cheese

¾ Cup Mayonnaise

1 Tbsp. Lemon Pepper

1 Tbsp. Minced Garlic

Place chicken breasts in a greased pan. Mix the rest of the ingredients together and pour over chicken breasts. Bake at 375 for one hour. Serve over brown rice. You can also add fresh or frozen broccoli to this dish before baking.

Blueberry & Cran-Raisin Salad

Bag of Salad Greens

Green Onions, chopped

Blueberries, Strawberries, or Mandarin Oranges

Bag Cran-Raisins

Rice Noodles   (Publix has them)

Feta Cheese

Pine Nuts

Mix ingredients together in large salad bowl. Add dressing at the last minute before serving.

Salad dressing - equal parts sugar, apple vinegar, and oil: mix all together, pour on salad last minute.

Buttermilk Biscuits

2 Cups Flour

3 Heaping tsp. Baking Powder

½ tsp Salt

2 Tbsp. Sugar

½ Cup Crisco Shortening

½ tsp. Baking Soda

1 Cup Buttermilk

Preheat oven to 450°F. Mix together the flour, baking powder, salt & sugar. Cut in the shortening using a pastry blender. Make a well in the center and pour baking soda and buttermilk in all at once, stirring together. Drop dough by big spoonfuls onto a lightly greased baking pan. Bake for 15 to 20 minutes, until tops are lightly browned.

Tunnel of Fudge Cake

1 ¾ Cup White Sugar	2 Cups Powdered Sugar
1 ¾ Cup Butter	6 Eggs
2 ¼ Cups Flour	¾ Cup Unsweetened Cocoa

2 Cups Chopped Walnuts (measure after chopping)

Preheat oven to 350°. Grease and flour Bundt pan. In a large bowl, cream butter & sugar until light and fluffy. Add eggs one at a time. Beat thoroughly. Add powdered sugar, blending well. Add flour, cocoa, and chopped walnuts. Pour into greased and floured Bundt pan. Bake about 45 minutes—the top will be set and edges start to pull away from the sides of the Bundt pan. Cool for 2 hours; turn out onto pretty cake plate. Cool 2 more hours. Drizzle with glaze; let glaze run down sides of cake.

Glaze:

¾ Cup Powdered Sugar

¼ Cup Unsweetened Cocoa

4-6 teaspoons Milk

Combine ingredients. Add enough milk to make it drizzle!

One of my closest friends loves chocolate. I found this recipe for her birthday and everyone fell in love with it. It creates a "tunnel of fudge" while it bakes. (from Ella Rita Helfrich of Texas: 1966 Pillsbury Bake-Off Contest, second place.) Delicious! Don't skimp on the nuts or it won't work! One year, I took the cake out to early because the same friend (I was making it again!) wanted to go to the movies. When I tried to invert it onto my cake plate, it fell apart. I scooped it back up and put it back in the oven. That year it was a "maze of fudge" rather than a tunnel, but it was still delicious!

EZ Brownies with Peanut Butter Frosting

2 Packages Fudge Brownie Mix, prepared & baked according to package directions, except adding: 1 Cup White Chocolate Chips and 1 Cup Semi-Sweet Chocolate Chips before baking!

1 Cup Peanut Butter

1 Cup XXX Sugar

4-6 Tbsp. Milk

When brownies have cooled, combine peanut butter, XXX sugar, and milk in a small bowl, blending by hand until smooth. Frost brownies generously!

Frozen Lemon Cream

1 Can (1⅔ Cup) Evaporated Milk, Thoroughly Chilled

¾ Cup Sugar

3 Tbsp. Lemon Juice

12 Graham Crackers, Crumbled & Divided

Beat evaporated milk until stiff. Slowly add sugar then lemon juice. Beat until very stiff. Spread half of the graham cracker crumbs in the bottom of a 9"x9" pan. Pour in cream. Add remaining crumbs. Cover tightly and freeze until ready to serve.

Hospitality to Strangers!

Love spills over from loved ones to strangers as we practice hospitality faithfully. I remember my mother volunteering at the state hospital with mentally ill patients. She began having them over, four at a time, for lunches. When she had made it through each patient, she thought it would be fun to have the whole ward over to the house for an Easter Egg Hunt. The hospital brought them over in a large van and the patients had a great time hunting for eggs. When it was time to go, though, two patients were missing. We found one at the bus stop and the other under my sister's bed. We both checked under each other's beds for months. Even so, how I appreciate my mother's heart for reaching out to those who were hurting, in trouble or poor! She was like the Proverbs 31 woman who "opens her arms to the poor and extends her hands to the needy (verse 20). All kinds of people dined at our table from wealthy business men to migrant farmers. My mother's love spilled over to strangers on a regular basis.

"Cal and Mimi frequently entertained wealthy, professional Ecuadorians in their home, with house staff suitable to what this entailed. But Mimi's heart was equally with the people around their table and the people in the streets. Their home, like the others around it, was encircled by high walls topped with broken glass or barbed wire. But every evening Mimi made sure that a plate of leftovers—not a paper plate, but a china plate with a napkin and utensils—was placed on a ledge just outside their back gate. The meal was always consumed. The plate, napkin, and utensils were always left in place" (Mary Beth Lagerborg, Dwelling: Living Fully from the Space you Call Home pg. 69, Fleming H Revel/Baker Publishing Group; 2007).

The Guest Room!

"And one thing more: Prepare a guest room for me, because I hope to be restored to you in answer to your prayers." The Apostle Paul writes to his friend and fellow believer, Philemon. (Philemon 1:22) Sometimes, God will have you host overnight company and you will need a guest room. If you are blessed to have a guest room, make it comfortable and cozy for whoever God brings your way.

If you are like us, with a big family, you will need to have a "guest room plan." Katie Beth's room was the designated guest room. Now Jenny Rose's bedroom is the family guest room. When we have overnight company, she moves out and company moves in. She leaves her room tidy, clears a space in her closet for guest to hang things, changes the bed linens, and puts out fresh towels. She is a wonderful hostess—that's why her room is the designated guest room!

To make guests comfortable, provide a comfortable place to sleep, a place to hang up clothes and, if possible, a drawer to store clothing. If you don't have a free drawer, give them a place to leave their suitcase on—a low dresser top or hope chest works great. It is nice to have a bright light for reading, an alarm clock for waking up, extra hangers in the closet for them to hang clothing, an extra blanket, and a Bible. Don't forget fresh sheets, clean towels, and a box of tissues. Consider making up a little basket with fresh fruit, bottled waters, and some snacks to put by the bedside. Also keep a file of local sites and attractions for out-of-town guests. Point them to the refrigerator, coffee pot, bathroom, and computer. Encourage them to make themselves at home. Keep offering your guests drinks, snacks and opportunities for activity until you are sure that they are comfortable enough to fix themselves a snack or cup of coffee. Some guests settle in more easily than others.

God has led us to invite people to stay with us for more extended times. At this point, they stop being guests, and are simply members of the household. To live with our family, we make sure that the relationship is beneficial for our "guest" and everyone in our family. "Guests" must abide by the household rules that the Curtis family abides by and pull their own weight with household chores. We usually have people who live with us contribute a little toward food, but have not needed the extra money. To have someone move in to help out financially becomes a little more of a formal situation, and that's another teaching.

Overnight Company Pumpkin Muffins

2 Large Eggs

1 ½ Cups Flour

1 Cup Canned Pumpkin

2 tsp. Baking Powder

½ Cup Milk

2 tsp. Pumpkin Pie Spice

1/3 Cup Butter, melted

½ tsp. Salt

1/4 Cup Sugar

½ Cup Nuts

½ Cup Brown Sugar

½ Cup Raisins

Beat together eggs, pumpkin, milk, and melted butter. Combine dry ingredients. Add liquid ingredients to dry ingredients all at once. Add raisins and nuts. Bake for 25 minutes at 400°F.

Overnight Company Breakfast in a Blanket

1 8 oz. Can Refrigerated Crescent Dinner Rolls

8 oz. Roll Pork Sausage

5 Large Eggs

1 Tbsp. Butter

1 Cup Shredded Monterey Jack Cheese

1 Cup Shredded Sharp Cheddar Cheese

½ Cup Green Pepper, chopped

½ Cup Onion, chopped

Salt & Pepper to Taste

Brown sausage in a 9" skillet over medium heat, crumble and drain. Scramble 4 eggs in butter in 9" skillet over medium heat.

Divide crescent roll dough into 4 rectangles. Roll out into 4"x6" rectangles and place on an ungreased cookie sheet.

Place ¼ of the sausage, ¼ of scrambled eggs, ¼ of cheeses, ¼ of green peppers, and ¼ of onion in the center of one dough piece. Add salt and pepper. Pull each corner of dough to the center and pinch seams closed. Repeat with each dough piece.

Beat remaining egg and brush the pastry tops with the beaten egg.

Bake at 375°F for 13 minutes or until golden brown.

Let the Little Children Come to Me

Jesus' disciples tried to shoo the children away, but Jesus took them in his arms and blessed them. Let's be adults who take children in our hearts and bless them. Welcome children into your homes with glad hearts. Some of my happiest memories are of adults who showed hospitality to me, including my grandparents.

Welcome children, just as you would adults, by standing up and greeting them by name with a hug. Offer them a drink and visit with them. Ask them about school, friends, and favorite pastimes. Treat them with kindness and respect.

When I was a little girl, one of the special things my grandmother, Beezie, did with me was to have tea. She would get out her china teapot and a crystal plate filled with cookies. Then came my favorite part, I got to pick out a teacup. Which one would I choose? They were all so delicate and beautiful. I had to be very careful with them. I felt like a grown-up lady having tea with my grandmother. What child can resist making cookies with grandma? If you have grandchildren, bake with them or teach them a skill such as knitting or sewing. My mom taught Katie Beth and Jenny Rose how to knit. My grandmother taught me to crochet. Make memories with your children, grandchildren and other people's children.

Children's Favorite Candy Sushi

1 ½ Tbsp. Butter, cut into pieces

18 Regular Marshmallows

3 Cups Rice Krispies Cereal

6 Fruit Roll-Ups

24 Gummy Worms

Melt butter in a medium saucepan over low heat and add marshmallows. Stir marshmallows until completely melted. Remove mixture from heat and add cereal. Stir to coat cereal evenly in melted marshmallows.

Roll out the fruit roll-ups. Place equal amounts of the coated cereal onto each fruit roll up and spread evenly across the fruit roll up leaving a small ½" tab of fruit roll up on one edge. Place 2 gummy worms at the opposite edge of the coated cereal mixture from the tab. (Use two more if needed to have double worms the full length of the roll up.) Wrap and roll the candy and fruit, until the cereal wraps completely around the worms and the tab can be overlapping the fruit wrap. Repeat with remaining rolls.

Children's Favorite EZ Chocolate Fondue

3 Chocolate Bars

2 Tbsp. Whipping Cream

Place ingredients in fondue pot and allow them to simmer until melted and smooth.

Arrange an assortment of bite-sized dipping foods on a lazy Susan around fondue pot. Some suggestions are strawberries, bananas, apples, grapes, cherries, pound cake, marshmallows, raisins and shelled nuts. Spear with fondue forks or wooden skewers, dip, swirl and   enjoy!

Homemade Pancake Syrup

2 Cups Sugar

2 Cups Water

¼ tsp. Salt

1 tsp. Maple Flavoring

Boil sugar and water for five minutes. Add salt and maple flavoring. Store in refrigerator. Reheat as needed.

 **EZ Fruity Macaroons**

4 Cups Flaked Coconut

1 Can (14 oz.) Sweetened Condensed Milk

½ tsp. Almond Extract

1 Package (3 oz.) Strawberry or Cherry Gelatin

In large bowl, combine all ingredients and mix thoroughly. Cover and refrigerate at least 2 hours. Spoon into 1" balls and bake at 350 for 8-10 minutes.

More Thoughts on Hospitality!

Here are some more thoughts on hospitality from Emilee Barnes.

"A welcoming home is a place of refuge, a place where people worn down by the noise and turmoil and hostility of the outside world can find a safe resting place. A welcoming home is a place that you and others can enjoy coming home to" (Emilee Barnes, Spirit of Loveliness page 15, Harvest House Publishers; 1992).

"Here's another unmistakable mark of a welcoming home. It's an expression of you. A welcoming home is one that reflects the spirit and personalities of the people who make it. This means that if your home and your life look and feel just like mine, one of us has a problem. Your home should be uniquely and beautifully you. It should reflect your own special and personal spirit of loveliness....A welcoming home is a reflection of everyone who lives there. Part of its charm is the sense of diverse personalities merging to create a unique environment" (Emilee Barnes, *Spirit of Loveliness* page 18, Harvest House Publishers; 1992).

"The spirit of welcome begins in your own heart, in your own attitudes. It has its birth in your willingness to accept yourself as God's child and to be grateful for your place in God's family, your true spiritual home. With that foundation, welcome becomes a way of life. You open your life to others instead of shutting them out. You learn to see your encounters with people as gifts instead of viewing them as hindrances and distractions. And you treasure your close relationships for what they are—gifts from God. With that attitude, a smile and a hug become as important to the spirit of welcome as a candle and a pot of stew" (Emilee Barnes, *Spirit of Loveliness* page 19, Harvest House Publishers; 1992).

"Most important, a welcoming home is a place of blessing—a place where you are made aware of God's blessing and through which you can pass on His blessing to others," (Emilee Barnes, Spirit of Loveliness page 19, Harvest House Publishers; 1992).

12 HOME: A WELCOME CENTER & A CELEBRATION CENTER

Imagine if houses could talk! What would they say to each other? Let's find out!

On Bluebell Lane, there are five houses that wait until their families fall asleep to talk each night. Victoria is a beautiful blue and white farm house with a wrap-around porch and gingerbread trim. Anna is a brick Colonial with black shutters. Brittany is a sleek modern home and Betsy, a log cabin. The final home is a cute yellow bungalow named Bonnie. Though having startling different personalities, the houses enjoy talking to one another each night, especially talking about their families.

"Dad got home yesterday and the family was thrilled," Betsy shared happily.

"Where did he go?" Bonnie asked curiously. Her family never went anywhere.

"Paris this time...on business," Betsy replied.

"Business? Right, and I have a bridge I can sell you," Brittany replied sarcastically. Her family was just a married couple with no children. It was her fifth marriage and his third.

"Why can't you ever trust people?" Victoria asked sadly.

"Well, not everyone can have the perfect family," Anna snapped. Her family homeschooled, so everything was always noisy and messy. Her family's dad had just lost his job and things were tense. He had even asked his wife why they had so many children, anyway. As if it were his wife's fault. Anna kept that to herself. She was worried.

"Paris must be romantic this time of year," Victoria mused.

"How would you know?" Anna snapped again. "You've never left Bluebell Lane." Victoria had the perfect family in Anna's mind. Both parents had well-paying jobs, the children went to private schools, and the furniture was right out of a magazine. They even had a maid and a gardener. Victoria was always in perfect shape, just like the mom in the family, who still looked like a college co-ed.

"I know about Ken losing his job," Victoria admitted to Anna.

"How did you find out?" Anna felt some relief that someone else knew.

"The maid goes to your family's church and she prays for them," Victoria smiled sweetly with her perfect blue shutters. "Your family will be fine!"

"How can you be sure?" Anna asked, feeling afraid.

"There is so much laughter and hugging that goes on inside your walls…so much real living."

Anna nodded, glancing down at the crack in her window where Billy had not quite broken it with his baseball, and the fingerprints on her sliding glass door. There were weeds in the garden too. But Victoria was right. There was a lot of love inside her walls even though the furniture was old and torn.

"I think that they'll make it too," Anna smiled. "But, of course, they'll never be like your family."

"They don't ever want to be like my family," Victoria admitted for the first time. All the other houses looked at her.

"But you are so beautiful and your family seems so perfect," little Bonnie gasped.

"Yes, beautiful garden, lovely furniture, and a beautiful Christmas family photograph. I am sad to tell you that this house is not a dwelling place. Real life doesn't take place inside my walls. I look good on the outside, but inside it's just too quiet."

"God can change things," Bonnie piped up.

"Who is God?" Brittany asked. "I've never heard of him.

"He's a builder," Betsy spoke in a quiet, but firm voice. "He's an Architect, a Great Builder, an Interior Designer, and a Fixer of Broken Dreams.

"Well, Victoria, there's your answer!" Brittany agreed. There was really nothing more to say.

Read Proverbs 14:1

Just a reminder that a woman builds her house with wisdom: hard work, love for her family, kindness, integrity, faith in God, frugalness, modesty, speaking with wisdom, and managing her home.

Conversely, a foolish woman tears her home down with nagging, greed, unwholesome words, anger, immodesty, talking too much, laziness, and ignoring God and God's ways.

Our home is a welcome center and a celebration center. Think for a minute about what that would entail. What are your thoughts on this? What would a welcome center look like? What would a celebration center look like?

A Welcome Center is

A Celebration Center is

In both cases—life & love are shared, memories are made, and relationships are strengthened!

A Welcome Center

God Welcomes people to Heaven! Those lovely gates (made out of single pearls) are wide open. God's Presence fills Heaven. He invites His children in to fellowship with Him. Remember when we talked about abiding? Jesus invites us right **now** to abide in Him.

When we abide in Jesus, we accept His invitation and receive His welcome. As we abide, His Presence fills our hearts and lives. Through us, His Holy Spirit invites others to "come in" and welcomes them when they accept our invitation and receive our welcome. If we are abiding in Jesus, then Jesus welcomes people through us. His love flows through us to the world around us: our family, friends, and, even, strangers.

Abiding is related to hospitality because the same ideas of welcome and being at home in someone's love exist. Abiding in Jesus is making yourself at home **in** Him. Hospitality is inviting people to **abide** in your home, love, and life. We extend our arms to welcome in those whom the Lord has called us to love.

Read I Timothy 5:1-10

How is Timothy to treat older men?

What behavior should characterize Timothy's relationships with older women?

How should Timothy behave with younger women?

Other believers are really our family! If we want to understand how we should interact with other believers, then get a book on family life and apply what you read to your relationships in the church. The Body of Christ is our **forever family.**

Describe what younger widows should do after they are finished grieving.

Describe God's plan to take care of older widows.

What happens in the local church if older widows don't have children, grandchildren, or other family members to care for them?

It seems that widows without family members are involved somehow in ministry with the church and, in return, the church supports these older widows. Because of the work involved, or for some undisclosed reason, the older widows have to meet certain criteria. One is that they have been faithful to their husbands.

What are the other criteria for widows receiving church support?

If this is how widows are chosen to receive support from the church, these qualifications must be standards that apply to all women who are serious about their commitment to the Lord.

Look carefully at this passage and think about the women you know. Does this passage remind you of any godly women who are living out these requirements for the widows?

Women I know	How they live out this passage!

If you look carefully at this passage, you will see that much of this ministry takes place in and from the home. Hospitality places a big part in New Testament Christianity. Home is a place where ministry begins.

Look at this *Circle of Good Deeds*. Let's start in the center and label the good deeds listed moving from the center outward through the concentric circles.

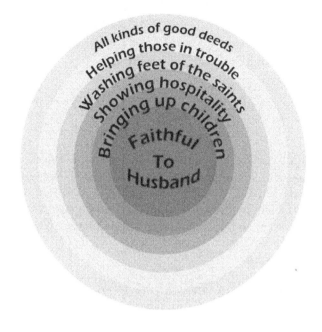

All kinds of good deeds
Helping those in trouble
Washing feet of the saints
Showing hospitality
Bringing up children
Faithful
To
Husband

Good Deeds:

Bringing up c_____.

Hospitality I: S_____.

Hospitality II: W_____.

Hospitality III: H_____.

Hospitality IV & Beyond: A_____.

Hospitality is a powerful ministry because it involves serving, family living, and fun. We enjoy building relationships and spending time together. That is fun in itself, but we also grow in the Lord when we spend time with other believers. Hard work is another aspect of hospitality that cannot be overlooked. Serving others through hospitality brings glory to God, but it also builds godly character in every family member.

Read I Peter 5:14

What command does Peter give to his readers?

This is the Spirit of Welcome! Greeting communicates welcome, acceptance, and a promise of more to come. So many people want the church to hold out hope for their tomorrows. Greeting communicates hope to people that there are people in this world that accept them and possible friendships lay ahead. What a lonely world we live in! How wonderful a warm greeting works to warm hearts and lift spirits.

Mae, a young friend of mine, is quick to greet people, no matter how young or old. She gets to church early with her family and when she sees people pull up in the parking lot, she runs to greet them. She is serving God by greeting His people with warmth and genuine acceptance.

A Celebration Center

Read Psalm 145:4-7

How does one generation commend God's works to the next generation?

One Generation commends God's works to the next generation and the one after that in the following ways:

- Speaking of God's splendor and majesty to their children and grandchildren
- Testifying of God's might acts and intervention in their lives

- Celebrating God's incredible goodness!

One Generation instills values in the next generation and the one after that in the following ways:

- Speaking of God's splendor and majesty to their children and grandchildren
- Testifying of God's mighty acts and intervention in their lives
- Celebrating God's incredible goodness!

Holidays are the perfect time to talk about God, share testimonies of His miracles, and celebrate with glad hearts. Family stories can be told. Testimonies can be recalled. Family traditions can make celebrations special and provide memories that will last a lifetime!

It's always time to celebrate!

Family Traditions: Renewing our Minds!

Christmas and other holiday traditions are dear to many of us, but as we grow in the Lord, we want our traditions to more accurately reflect our growing faith and maturity in Christ.

Traditions are set patterns that constitute a way of life, past down from generation to generation. Some traditions are inherently evil, such as getting drunk on New Year's Eve and some traditions are inherently good, such as going to church every Sunday as a family. Many traditions are neutral.

We need to examine the traditions we keep and make sure that, first of all, they are not ungodly. If they are worldly or sinful, they need to be discarded. Then, we need to be proactive in our selection of what traditions we will adopt.

Family traditions can instill values and establish a unique identity for your family as your family celebrates God's goodness and mercy. We want to choose specific ways to celebrate in our homes. Don't underestimate the value of family traditions in our celebration centers.

"Bob and I have had such fun establishing traditions in our family. One of the most meaningful began on our first Christmas together—my very first Christmas as a Christian. Money was tight that year, but we managed a tree, and we gave each other ornaments. And we continued to give each other ornaments in the following years. When the children were born, they got ornaments too. (Years later, when Jenny got married at age 22, we gave Jenny and Craig 22 ornaments to start their own tree.) And the tradition continues as our family grows. A few years ago, I decided not to give ornaments; after 33 years I thought nobody cared. How wrong I was! Everybody was so disappointed that I went out first thing on December 26 and found just the right ornaments to continue the tradition. And that practice of giving ornaments, begun by Bob and me on our first Christmas together, still warms our hearts when we gather together year after year." (Emilee Barnes, *Spirit of Loveliness* page 19, Harvest House Publishers; 1992).

Bob and Emilee's family know that in their family, everyone gets an ornament at Christmas. This provides a sense of family identity for everyone in the family. Yes, it is simple, but that is what is so wonderful about traditions—they are simple, yet powerful tools for building our homes.

Celebrating God's Goodness!

Traditions can be wonderful tools for your family to celebrate God's goodness; to instill values; to establish a unique identity for your family; to provide security; and to build memories.

"The joy of the Lord is my strength." (Nehemiah 8:10) is a verse we often quote; but did you know that the context of that verse is celebrating the Lord's goodness with feasting? Look up that passage and see for yourself. When you read about the *sweet drinks* and *choice foods* they were asked to enjoy, it will remind you of eggnog, hot chocolate, Christmas cookies, and cinnamon rolls. Hmmm…it's beginning to sound a lot like….

Holiday Traditions Instill Values

We have the great privilege as parents to train our children to walk with God and to walk in all His ways.

Traditions are the perfect time to instill values in a positive, fun way. What fun to learn to honor parents by serving them breakfast in bed or giving them beautifully wrapped presents on Mother's Day or Father's Day. How nice to learn the importance of thankfulness by sharing praise reports around the table before indulging in a delicious meal. What a blast to have patriotism taught by acting out skits about our country's heritage while wearing red, white, and blue.

Each holiday can have a specific thing that we celebrate and specific values and Biblical principles that we strive to instill.

Ask other Christian families what they do to instill values in their children during the holidays. You may discover a gem that you want to try in your own home.

For more ideas on holidays & traditions…

joyfulandsuccessfulhomeschooling.com/traditions.aspx

Annie's Page

annieshomepage.com/index.html

For holiday & special occasion menus & for more recipes…

joyfulandsuccessfulhomeschooling.com/recipes.aspx

New Years

"For I know that plans I have for you,' declares the Lord, 'plans for welfare and not for calamity to give you a future and a hope"' (Jeremiah 29:11 NASB)

Celebrate: Our hope for the future in Christ

Values: Reflection; Examination; Goal setting

Traditions to Establish Family Identity:

Special family meal and/or dessert

Family prayer meeting with worship & communion at midnight

Everyone share God's greatest blessing for past year & one way God answered prayer.

Make goals for the coming year. Pray for one another.

Holiday Cheese Ball

8 oz. Soft Cream Cheese

2 Cups Sharp Shredded Cheddar Cheese

1 Envelope Onion Soup Mix

Mix ingredients together; roll into a ball. Chill. Serve with crackers.

Valentines' Day

"Marriage is to be held in honor among all, and the marriage bed is to be undefiled" (Hebrews 13:4 NASB)

Celebrate: God's gift of love and marriage.

Values: Honor marriage.

Traditions to Establish Family Identity:

Decorate with roses and hearts.

Let the children bake heart-shaped cookies.

Read Bible love stories: David & Abigail; Ruth and Boaz; Isaac and Rebekah.

Pray for married couples in the church.

Exchange love/appreciation notes.

Eat a fancy dinner by candlelight while Mom and Dad share the story of their courtship and marriage.

Wedding Breakfast Strawberry Soup

4 Cups Strawberries, cleaned and capped

1 Cup Orange Juice

½ tsp Cinnamon

¼ Cup Sugar

1 Cup Plain Yogurt or Buttermilk

Puree ingredients in a blender. Serve chilled. Makes 4 servings.

Easter

"I am the resurrection and the life. He who believes in me will live even if he dies; and everyone who lives and believes in Me will never die" (John 11:25, 26 NASB)

Celebrate: Jesus' resurrection and eternal life.

Values: Newness, renewing, rebirth, hope for Heaven.

Traditions to Establish Family Identity:

Have a family sunrise service.

Attend church together in new dresses or matching outfits.

Act out the Easter story, or read it together or watch a movie on the life of Jesus.

Decorate with spring colors: green, yellow, pink, and lavender.

Hide plastic eggs filled with candy, let children find eggs and empty candy; then they put resurrection symbols inside and hide them for the adults.

Share the Gospel with your children and invite them to become Believers.

Easter Carrot Cake

2 Cups Flour

2 Cups Sugar

1 ½ Cups Oil

2 tsp. Soda

2 tsp. Salt

2 tsp. Cinnamon

3 Cups Grated Carrots

4 Large Eggs

Preheat oven to 350°F. Grease and flour a 3 round cake pans. Mix dry ingredients, then add cooking oil and stir well. Add carrots, each egg one at a time, and mix well. Pour into 3 round cake pans. Bake at 350°F for 25 minutes.

Cream Cheese Frosting

1 Box XXX Sugar

1 (8 oz.) Package Cream Cheese

1 Stick Butter, melted

2 tsp Vanilla

1 Cup Coconut

1 Cup Pecans

Melt butter and add XXX sugar to it. Beat until smooth; add softened cream cheese. Beat again until smooth. Mix in vanilla. Frost cake on tops, bottoms, and sides, putting it all together. Sprinkle cake with coconut and pecans.

Mothers' and Fathers' Days

"Honor your father and mother, which is the first commandment with a promise, that it may go well with you and that you may live long on the earth" (Ephesians 6:2, 3 NASB)

Celebrate: God's gift of parents.

Values: Honoring parents.

Traditions to Establish Family Identity:

Breakfast in bed.

Cards, flowers and phone calls to Dad, Mom and grandparents.

Fix favorite meals or take to favorite restaurant.

Talk about fatherly aspects of God on Father's Day/motherly aspects of God on Mothers' Day.

Dad gets his favorite deserts for seven nights in a row---different ones. Mom gets chocolate.

Breakfast in Bed Egg Scramble

Cheese Sauce: 2 Tbsp. butter, melted & stir in 2 Tbsp. flour, then add 2 Cups warm milk, salt & pepper & 1 Cup grated cheddar cheese.

1 Cup Diced Canadian Bacon

¼ Cup Scallions

12 Eggs, beaten

3 Tbsp. Butter

¼ lb. Mushrooms

1 Recipe Cheese Sauce

4 Tbsp. Melted Butter

2 Cups Bread Crumbs

¼ tsp. Paprika

Cook Canadian bacon & scallions in 3 Tbsp. butter. Add eggs & scramble until set. Fold eggs and mushrooms into cheese sauce. Turn mixture into a greased baking dish. Sprinkle bread crumbs over the top, drizzle 4 Tbsp. melted butter, paprika over that. Cover and chill overnight in refrigerator. Take out 30 minutes before baking. Bake uncovered 350°F for 30 minutes (or 45 maybe). Great for a brunch party.

Fourth of July

"Righteousness exalts a nation, but sin is a disgrace to any people" (Proverbs 14:34 NASB)

Celebrate: Freedom to serve God, Christian heritage.

Values: Patriotism, appreciation for freedom.

Traditions to Establish Family Identity:

Fly your flag outside.

Discuss Declaration of Independence, Constitution, and godly founding fathers.

Make up skits about historical events.

Watch fireworks display and sing patriotic songs.

Decorate with red, white, and blue and eat traditional American foods.

Chuck Wagon Beans

1 Pound Bacon, fried and crumbled	1½ Cloves Garlic, minced
2 Pounds Ground Beef	1½ Cups Ketchup
3 Cups Chopped Onions	3 Tbsp. Prepared Mustard
1 Cup Finely Chopped Celery	Salt & Pepper to Taste
1 Giant Size Can Bush's Baked Beans	

Preheat oven to 375°F. Brown ground beef with onions and celery. Stir in garlic, ketchup, mustard, beans, salt and pepper. Bake covered 1 hour 15 minutes or simmer in crock-pot.

Reformation Day *(10/31)*/*All Saints Day*
(11/1)

"And all these, having gained approval through their faith …
Therefore, since we have such a great cloud of witnesses
surrounding us, let us also lay aside every encumbrance and the sin
which so easily entangles us, and let us run with endurance race
that is set before us" (Hebrews 11:39-12:1 NASB)

Celebrate: Our Christian Heritage & History.

Values: Courage, Standing firm for the Truth, Making Disciples.

Traditions to Establish Family Identity:

Heroes for Jesus Party

Learn about Martin Luther/ 95 Thesis/ Wittenburg Door

Act out the story of Martin Luther or another Christian hero

Watch a movie about Martin Luther or another Christian hero

Make a church history timeline

Laura's Pumpkin Custard

2 Eggs	1 Cup Sugar
1 tsp. Salt	1 tsp. Vanilla
1 tsp. Cinnamon	3 Tbsp. Flour
3 Tbsp. Butter, softened	3/4 Cup Milk
1 Large (28 oz.) Can Pumpkin	Cool Whip

Using electric mixer, combine ingredients, except cool whip, until
well blended. Pour custard into casserole dish. Bake, uncovered, at
350°F for 50 minutes. Top with Cool Whip when serving. Serve
hot or cold.

Thanksgiving

"In everything, give thanks" (I Thessalonians 5:18 NASB)

Celebrate: God's abundant blessings.

Values: Gratefulness, praise.

Traditions to Establish Family Identity:

Tell the story of the first Thanksgiving.

Everyone share what they are thankful for and thank Jesus!

Invite friends over for a Praise Breakfast---share testimonies and follow with a time of worship.

Contribute food or deliver food baskets to the needy.

Invite those without family to share holiday.

Decorate with horn of plenty, fruits and vegetables, autumn leaves, baskets, pilgrims, Indians and turkeys.

Eat traditional meal and try to include foods from the original Thanksgiving feast.

Steve Smith's Sweet Potato Pie

1 Pre-Baked 9-inch Pie Crust

2 Sweet Potatoes, baked

1 Cup Dark Brown Sugar, packed

½ tsp. Salt

1 tsp. Ground Cinnamon

¼ tsp. Grated Nutmeg

2 tsp. Ground Ginger

¾ Cup Half-n-Half

4 Large Eggs, beaten

½ Cup Half-n-Half

1 Cup Heavy Cream

¼ Cup Maple Syrup

Preheat oven to 350°F. Place the oven rack on the lowest level. In a large size sauce pan, stir together the sweet potato purée, sugar, salt, cinnamon, nutmeg, ginger and the three quarters of a cup of the half-and-half over medium heat. When the mixture is steaming hot, transfer it to a food processor fitted with a metal blade; blend until smooth. Combine the eggs with the remaining half-and-half. With the food processor motor running, blend the egg mixture with the sweet potato. Pour the warm filling into your prepared pie shell and bake until the center is firm and the surface has browned and cracked slightly, about 50-60 minutes. Let the pie cool for an hour or two before serving. Meanwhile whip the heavy cream to soft peaks in a mixing bowl. Add the maple syrup and continue to whip until stiff peaks form. Chill until ready to serve. Top each slice of pie with the maple whipped cream just before serving.

Christmas

"For God so loved the world that He GAVE His only begotten Son—that whosoever believes in Him will not perish, but have everlasting life!" (John 3:16)

Celebrate: God's gift of salvation through His Son, Jesus!

Values: Giving

Traditions to Establish Family Identity:

Decorate Christmas Tree

Christmas Family Devotions

Christmas Unit Studies instead of regular school

Make a baby layette for Jesus and give to a Crisis Pregnancy Center

Invite those without family to share holiday.

Decorate with red & green, angels, stars, velvet bows, teddy bears, candles, manger scenes, stockings, bells, and family heirlooms.

Traveling Dinner on Christmas Eve

Sing "Happy Birthday" to Jesus on Christmas morning

Eat traditional meals

Baba's Cranberry Bread

2 Cups Flour

1 Cup Sugar

1 ½ tsp. Baking Powder

½ tsp Baking Soda

1 tsp. Salt

¼ Cup Shortening

¾ Cup Orange Juice

1 Tbsp. Grated Orange Peel

1 Egg, well beaten

½ Cup Chopped Nuts

1 ½ Cups Cranberries

Sift together flour, sugar, baking powder, soda, and salt. Cut in shortening. In a separate bowl, combine orange juice, peel, and egg. Add to flour mixture and blend well. Add ½ cup chopped nuts and cranberries. Pour into greased loaf pans and bake at 350°F for 1 hour.

Birthdays

"For You formed my inward parts, You wove me in my mother's womb. I will give thanks to You, for I am fearfully and wonderfully made" (Psalm 139:13, 14 NASB).

Celebrate: God's gift of birthday person.

Values: Self-esteem, honoring others.

Traditions to Establish Family Identity:

Make everyone's birthday special with their favorite meals, parties, gifts, etc.

Share why we are thankful for the birthday person and thank Jesus for them.

Pray over birthday person.

Look at baby book or baby pictures.

EZ Birthday Ice Cream Cake

1 Stick Butter

1 Package Oreo Sandwich Cookies

1 Gallon Cookies and Cream Ice Cream

1 Small Container Cool Whip

Melt butter in oven at 350° in a 9" x13" baking pan. Crumble cookies into crumbs and mix with melted butter to make a crust. Spoon ice cream over crust. Spread Cool Whip on top for final layer.

You can substitute all kinds of cookies and ice cream flavors. Here are some favorites: chocolate chip cookies with cookie dough ice cream; mint Oreos with mint chocolate chip ice cream; and Nutter Butter cookies with peanut butter chocolate ice cream! Yummy!

Graduations

"Render to all what is due them: tax to whom tax is due; custom to whom custom; fear to whom fear; honor to whom honor" (Romans 13:7 NASB)

Celebrate: God's gift of birthday person.

Values: Hard work, completing a task

Traditions to Establish Family Identity:

Make a scrapbook of school years

Graduation ceremony and party

"Roast" the graduate

Family pray over graduate after he shares his dreams and plans for the future

Make a slide show of graduate from birth to graduation

Everyone share what they admire and appreciate about the graduate

Make a "wisdom book" where everyone writes a verse that applies to the graduate and God's will

Cajun Crab Dip

½# Sea Legs	3 Tbsp. Hot Sauce
8 oz. Cream Cheese	2 Tbsp. Lemon Juice
1 Bunch Green Onions, chopped	¾ Cup Mayonnaise

Mix all ingredients together. Serve chilled on wheat crackers.

Meredith Curtis

RESOURCES

On the following pages there are resources that you can use to grow in abiding and homemaking.

Resources for Dwelling!

Abide in Christ by Andrew Murray

The Christian's Secret of a Happy Life by Hannah Whitall Smith

The Vine Life by Colleen Townsend Evans

Secrets of the Vine by Bruce Wilkinson; Multnomah; 2006

Lovely to Behold by Meredith Curtis; Powerline Productions

A Wise Woman Builds by Meredith Curtis; Powerline Productions

The Hidden Art of Homemaking by Edith Schaeffer; Tyndale House; 1985.

L'Abri by Edith Schaeffer

What is a Family? by Edith Scaeffer

Disciplines of a Beautiful Woman by Anne Ortlund

Improving Your Serve: The Art of Unselfish Living by Charles Swindoll

The Blessing by Gary Smalley and John Trent; Pocket Books; 1990.

Simple Secrets of a Beautiful Home: Creating a Place You and Your Family will Love by Emilie Barnes; Harvest House; 2004.

Home Warming: Secrets to Making Your Home a Welcoming Place by Emilie Barnes; Harvest House; 2005.

If Teacups Could Talk by Emilie Barnes; Harvest House.

Open Heart, Open Home by Karen Burton Mains; Intervarsity Press; 2002.

A Life that Says Welcome: Simple Ways to Open Your Heart and Home to Others by Karen Ehman; Baker; 2006.

Dwelling: Living Fully From the Space You Call Home by Mary Beth Lagerborg; Fleming H. Revel; 2007.

Welcome Inn: Practicing the Art of Hospitality in Jesus' Name by Meredith Curtis; Powerline Productions

Romancing Your Child's Heart by Monte Swan; Loyal; 2000.

Creating Family Traditions: Let's Make a Memory Series by Shirley Dobson and Gloria Gaither; Multnomah; 2004.

Hide it in your Heart: Let's Make a Memory Series by Shirley Dobson and Gloria Gaither; Multnomah; 2004.

Celebrating Special Times with Special People: Let's Make a Memory Series by Shirley Dobson and Gloria Gaither; Multnomah; 2004.

God's Girls Friendship, Traditions, & Celebrations Course by Meredith Curtis; Powerline Productions

Homeschooling at the Speed of Life: Balancing Home, School, and Family in the Real World by Marilyn Rockett; B & H Publishing Group; 2007.

Joyful and Successful Homeschooling by Meredith Curtis; Powerline Productions

Seven R's of Homeschooling by Meredith Curtis; Powerline Productions

Quick & EZ Unit Study Fun! by Meredith Curtis; Powerline Productions

Websites for Dwelling

Joyful and Successful Homeschooling, Home Sweet Home
joyfulandsuccessfulhomeschooling.com/hsh.html

Annie's Holiday Page
annieshomepage.com/holiday.html

Taste of Home (yummy recipes!)
tasteofhome.com/

Master Your Money Ministries
masteryourmoney.com/

Crown Financial Ministries
crown.org/

Mary Hunt Debt-Proof Living
debtproofliving.com/

More Hours in my Day
mhimd.com/

Christian Homemaking
christian-homemaking.com

From Messed to Blessed/The House that Cleans Itself
thehousethatcleansitself.com/

Tips from Tulip
wwwtipsfromtulipcom.blogspot.com/

Focus on the Family
focusonthefamily.com/

Gary Chapman's Love Languages
5lovelanguages.com/

Tomorrow's Forefathers
brothersandsisters.net/

Being World Changers!
Raising World Changers!

Powerline Productions exists to serve you! We want you to grow in your relationship with Jesus, experience joy and success in your homeschooling journey, and fulfill the Great Commission with your family in your home, church, and community.

We offer Homeschooling books, unit studies, classes, high school classes, ladies Bible study workbooks, God's Girls Bible study workbooks, Real Men Bible study workbooks, Worship CDs, teaching CDs, DVDs, and cookbooks just for you!

Our Websites

joyfulandsuccessfulhomeschooling.com/
jshomeschooling.com/
finishwellcon.com/
powerlineprod.com/
meredithcurtis.com/

E-books Available @ powerlineprod.com/
mediaangels.com/index.php?main_page=index&cPath=1_19
currclick.com/browse/pub/247/Powerline-Productions

Contact Us: Laura@powerlinecc.com &
Meredith@powerlinecc.com &
PastorMike@powerlinecc.com

Powerline Productions
251 Brightview Drive Lake Mary, FL 32746

Ladies Bible Studies

The Word of God brings wisdom to woman in their roles as wives, mothers, homemakers, mentors, leaders, teachers, and businesswomen. Dig into Scripture and allow it to transform your life! Draw closer to Jesus and experience success as you walk in God's plan for your life!

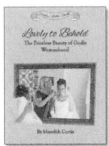

Maggie King Mysteries

If you like cozy mysteries, you will love this series! Meet Maggie King, a pastor's wife and homeschool mom who keeps stumbling across dead bodies. With her sidekicks, Sophia and Mary-Kate and her curious children, Maggie is on one adventure after another.

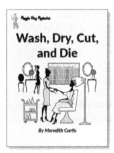
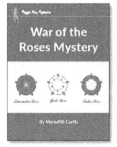
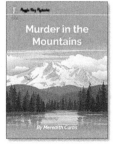

Books by Powerline Productions

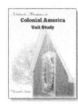  

About the Author

Meredith Curtis, a pastor's wife and homeschooling mom of five children, leads worship, mentors ladies, and, sometimes, even cooks dinner. Her passion is to equip people to love Jesus, raise godly children, and change the world around them with the power of the Gospel. "Lives are changed in the context of relationships," Meredith often says, as well as, "Be a world changer! Raise world changers!" She enjoys speaking to small and large groups.

You can find Meredith on her websites: MeredithCurtis.com, JSHomeschooling.com, PowerlineProd.com, FinishWellCon.com, and JoyfulandSuccessfulHomeschooling.com.

Meredith is the author of several books.
Joyful and Successful Homeschooling
Seven R's of Homeschooling
Quick & EZ Unit Study Fun
Unlocking the Mysteries of Homeschooling High School (with Laura Nolette)
Celebrate Thanksgiving
Teaching Writing in High School with Classes You Can Use
Teaching Literature in High School with Classes You Can Use
HIS Story of the 20th Century
HIS Story of the 20th Century for Little Folks

Meredith is the author of several cozy mysteries: The Maggie King Mysteries series.
Drug Dealers Deadly Disguise
Hurricanes Can Be Deadly
Legend of the Candy Cane Murder
Wash, Dry, Cut, & Die
War of the Roses Mystery
Murder in the Mountains

Meredith is the author of several Bible studies.
Lovely to Behold

A Wise Woman Builds
Jesus, Fill My Heart & Home
Welcome Inn: Practicing the Art of Hospitality in Jesus" Name
Friends to the End
God's Girls Beauty Secrets (with Sarah Jeffords)
God's Girls Friends to the End (with Katie-Beth Nolette & Sarah Jeffords)
God's Girls Talk about Boys, Dating, Courtship, & Marriage

Meredith is the author of several unit studies, timelines, and cookbooks.
Celebrate Christmas in Colonial America
Celebrate Christmas with Cookies
Travel to London
Celebrate Thanksgiving with the Pilgrims
American History Cookbook
Ancient History Cookbook
20th Century Cookbook (with Laura Nolette)
20th Century Timeline (with Laura Nolette)
American History Timeline (with Laura Nolette)
Ancient History (with Laura Nolette)

Meredith is the author of several high school classes.
American Literature and Research
British Literature and Writing
Who Dun It: Murder Mystery Literature & Writing
Communication 101: Essays and Speeches
Foundations of Western Literature
Economics, Finances, and Business
Worldview 101: Understand the Times
New Testament Survey
Old Testament Survey
Great Commission

And more…

Made in the USA
Las Vegas, NV
13 May 2021